I0820035
GHER BAND

RORY GALLA

Rory Gallagher

RY GALLAGHER
BAND
RANGEMASTER
VOX
VOX

GALLAGHER'S GUITARS

THE RORY GALLAGHER COLLECTION

TEXT BY JULIEN BITOUN
PHOTOGRAPHY BY ELEANOR JANE

CONTENTS

FOREWORD

It's All Treasure

Johnny Marr / London 2025

© Pat Graham

If you were ever at a Rory Gallagher concert, the first things you'd notice on the stage were his trusty old amplifiers—usually a 1960s Vox and a 1950s Fender. It was the mark of the man that, before he even appeared, you became aware that he had a vintage style—very deliberate, specific, and collectible. It was all part of his identity and his trade.

When he did make his entrance, he would already be holding his famous 1961 Fender Stratocaster, ready to go. There was no grand gesturing to the crowd, and no being attended to by a roadie presenting him with his instrument. He strode on, adjusted some switches on his amp, and then kicked off the show with a riff and a howl.

It was during one of these shows in the 1970s that I got my first glimpses of vintage instruments: a Martin D-35 acoustic guitar, a National Steel Dobro, and also a mandolin. These days we're more familiar with old instruments displayed as a conscious nod towards the past, but back in the days of giant shiny Marshall stacks and new wave keyboards, Rory's choice of instruments and equipment was unusual—and something of an education.

Decades later, I had the privilege of playing these instruments that were stored away—they are a poignant reminder of who Rory Gallagher was, a curated treasure trove that tells of passing time and a life of secret knowledge and sacred music. A lifetime of travel, expertise, and obsession that are now shared in this book.

First and foremost, Rory's love of unusual guitars was a sign of his passion as a fan. All of us who share this trait are powerless to resist the sight of a beautiful old acoustic or a lap steel from the 1930s—it's all treasure. Rory was a connoisseur, and as a seasoned professional he knew that the technology from the past was simply of better quality. This wasn't mere nostalgia—it was pragmatism born out of years of expertise and experience. He was also aware of the great mystical truth that some instruments you meet have music already "in them," and if you're lucky, they might give you a song or two—and sometimes a great one.

The love of the instruments is not the entire story for the guitar freak, though. There's the electricity, volume, and tone singing out from our beloved amplifiers, the look and design of which is another key aspect of the job and the vocation. They are marvelous things to use—exciting, technical, and also collectible. Are amplifiers merely machines? I don't think so—and neither did Rory. His classic amps told you something about him in the same way his choice of instruments did—his sneakers too.

The story of Rory Gallagher's life can be told through his music and what went into making it: dedication, passion, and obsession. Ireland, family, and the blues. Work, performance, and the road. And through his collection of instruments, we get the story of how he did what he did—and see the things he loved.

Introduction

For the Last Time

On July 8, 2024, the news made the headlines in the music press worldwide: the Rory Gallagher guitar collection was going to be put on sale at auction by Bonhams in London. After almost thirty years of being the instruments' custodian, Dónal Gallagher was getting ready to let go and let other people appreciate the instruments. As Rory's brother, former manager, and longtime confidant, Dónal is also the one who took over the legacy of Rory's music and made sure it would continue to touch people of all generations all over the world. He also enrolled his son Daniel on that mission. Since 2006, Daniel has overseen the production of numerous posthumous projects including the 2019 UK Top 20 album *Blues* and the recent *BBC Collection*.

On top of keeping Rory's music alive, Dónal and Daniel kept the guitar collection alive by having them played by fans, from enthusiastic unknowns to journalists to high-profile musicians like Joe Bonamassa, who played the '61 Strat on two songs at his March 2013 Royal Albert Hall show.

But the pressure became too much to bear. The '61 Strat, especially, is a blessing and a curse to own, given its value and status. Owning it means paying astronomical sums for insurance, security, and storage without ever having the chance to really enjoy it for what it is. Over the years, Dónal tried to set up arrangements to get the Strat into a museum that would display and care for it, but he never found a satisfactory deal.

When it was announced that the auction would be taking place, Sheena Crowley, daughter of Michael Crowley, who owned the store where Rory bought the Strat, launched a donation campaign to try to keep it in Cork, Ireland. The effort reached about €77,000 ($103,643), which remains a long stretch from the almost one million euros ($1,144,400) the Strat sold for on October 17, 2024. The good news is it was purchased by Live Nation Gaiety Ltd with the firm intention of keeping the Strat on Irish soil, as such it is being donated to the National Museum of Ireland. It will be on display at the museum in the 'Changing Ireland Galleries' as of October 2025.

Other of Rory's guitars sold for hefty sums, including the '58 Strat (€127,400 [$171,483]) and the D-35 (€102,000 [$137,294]), but the bulk of Rory's gear went between €5,000 and €15,000 ($6,730 and $20,190, respectively), which could almost be seen as reasonable prices compared with other guitar hero auctions of the same ilk.

Let's hope this means those instruments will keep on being played and enjoyed as they should. Rory would have wanted it that way.

1958–1970

Taste

ROGERS
the TASTE

The Early Years

Rory's First Guitar

Rory Gallagher was born in 1948 in Ballyshannon, a few miles from the border between Northern and Southern Ireland. A year later, his family crossed the border and settled in Northern Ireland, in Derry. Finally, when Rory was eight, the family, including Rory's little brother Dónal, moved to Cork near the southern shore. This is where Rory started to develop a taste for music. His father Danny played the accordion while his mother Monica was a singer and actress in a theater group, so it's fair to assume that Rory was exposed to music from a very early age without it necessarily being a conscious thing.

At the age of six, Rory had already heard the guitar in the hands of singing cowboys at the movies. Roy Rogers and Gene Autry were absolute superstars in the US who had turned a whole generation of youngsters into budding guitarists. In the 1950s, Ireland got the bug too. Rory discovered the early heroes of rock 'n' roll, which at the time was called rockabilly, especially Bill Haley & His Comets and Eddie Cochran. He also found something that spoke to him in the skiffle fad of the era with Lonnie Donegan and his main American influences, Lead Belly and Woody Guthrie. Through them, he finally got to the electric blues of Chuck Berry and (more than any other artist) Muddy Waters. That was the spark he needed, and from then on Rory wanted to become a musician.

First, he taught himself to play the ukulele, which was quite a common instrument in the UK at the time—a remnant of vaudeville culture, an Elvis Presley branded model from the Woolworths department store—but he moved on to a proper guitar at the age of nine. That guitar is depicted here sixty-eight years later, a witness to the first steps of one of the greatest electric blues players of all time. It is a steel-string acoustic, as opposed to nylon-string classical guitars that were prevalent among cheap instruments, and a flat-top, as opposed to the archtops that were standard for European manufacturers that had been brought up on violins and mandolins. There's no telling where it was made, but since there was no large guitar factory in Ireland at the time, it most likely came from somewhere else in Europe, maybe sold through a catalog. It has a twelve-fret neck like some of Rory's future acoustics and must have been an absolute treasure to a young budding artist at the time. It was certainly good enough to keep the spark alive.

Finding the Grail

1961 Fender Stratocaster

VOLUME
TONE
TONE

64851

Here we are. The show's main attraction, arriving very early in our timeline. For most great players, a first electric guitar is often just a fond memory, usually associated with epithets such as "unplaybable" or "wacky," to be polite. But not Rory: his first proper electric was the guitar of a lifetime, an instrument that he played so intensively for the remainder of his life that it became a crucial part of his persona. Long curly hair, check shirt, and battered sunburst Strat—that's all one needs to know to immediately think of Rory.

Very few guitar heroes keep a single main guitar for their whole career like Rory did from 1963 to 1995. Slash remains partial to his original Les Paul copies but uses a massive collection. Clapton had Blackie, but he only used it from 1970 to 1986. Gilmour had his Black Strat, but it only saw stage time from 1970 to 1986 (there must have been something in the air at the time), before bringing it out of retirement—and the Hard Rock Café—in 1997. Stevie Ray Vaughan comes close with his Number One Strat—another battered sunburst—but he had a nice collection. Brian May is one of those rare players that stuck to their original instrument for a lifetime of playing, and the fact that he built the Red Special himself with the help of his dad makes the story even more . . . well, special. Rory had a strong influence on May, which may have been an incentive for making the most out of a single tool.

A Choice Born of Necessity

Rory Gallagher bought his Strat in 1963 in Cork, at a place called Crowley's Music Store (named after owner Michael Crowley, no relation whatsoever with the dark wizard Aleister). American instruments were just starting to become part of the scenery in the UK, and you were much more likely to encounter one in London than in Ireland. In the immediate postwar years, imports from the other side of the pond were all but banned and so highly taxed that any instrument coming through would have been out of financial reach for any player. The situation got better in 1960, but even then, Fenders and Gibsons commanded prices that most budding players could not afford, making them objects of fantasy rather than obtainable instruments

Kids had to make do with the instruments they had, mostly unplayable archtops (try playing those Jimmy Reed licks on a German-made Framus). The lucky ones had proper solidbody electric guitars, but they were still funny-looking and-sounding European contraptions, made by the likes of Höfner in Germany, Eko in Italy, Hagström in Sweden, Egmond in the Netherlands, and Vox in the UK (which were actually made in Italy). Guitar players were kids, and the concept of shelling out a huge amount of cash for an instrument was only for professional musicians who needed the right tool for their trade. Even then, they usually had only one good guitar, as

the very notion of a collection was completely unimaginable back then.

Most UK players—and Rory was one of them—started out emulating Lonnie Donegan, a Scottish singer who started the *skiffle* craze. Skiffle is a musical genre mostly borrowed from the American folk music songbook but played with a Britishness. It's Lead Belly drinking tea, if you will. More important than the music itself was the DIY ethos conveyed by skiffle—the ideas that anybody can play an instrument, you don't need formal training or a proper guitar, and you can even build an instrument from scratch using a broomstick and a piece of rope. All that matters is having fun creating a sound with your friends. That philosophy went a long way in producing a generation of rock 'n' roll players in the UK, as future rock gods from Jimmy Page to Paul McCartney started out playing skiffle.

All the skiffle kids were playing archtop or flat-top acoustic guitars, so how did Rory get the idea to play a solidbody guitar? Even though he was heavily influenced by skiffle, Rory's knowledge of music ran deeper. He was aware of Buddy Holly and his weird-shaped guitar. But the main factor that brought him to the solidbody side was necessity. He was playing professionally at the age of fifteen, and at that time in Ireland the showband craze was in full swing. Those smaller orchestras featuring a brass section were playing the popular music of the day, including country, rock 'n' roll, early jazz, and indigenous material from the Celtic folk repertoire. Rory had joined the Fontana Showband in 1963, and he needed a professional instrument that could easily be amplified. Since Fontana only had six players, Rory had a lot of sonic real estate to fill up. That's when he saw the secondhand Strat in the window of Crowley's Music Store.

Strange Contraption

The Strat was arguably Leo Fender's masterpiece and remains an absolute bestseller to this day. The Telecaster came before, and it got a lot of things perfect even though it was a little crude (the old saying that "Leo got it right the first time" has a level of truth to it, of course), and the Jazzmaster came four years after the Strat, but it never turned into the Strat-killer it was supposed to be. It was too complicated and awkward to handle for its own good.

The Strat's contoured body is a model of perfection that's hard to beat for most guitar makers today. Every cut is where it should be, to the point that it feels like a well-worn pair of jeans. That's fitting in Rory's case, since his taste for blue denim left a blue hue on the back of the instrument.

The vibrato—or "synchronized tremolo," to quote Fender's official yet mistaken designation—is also a big part of the Strat's appeal, and it can be argued that most "modern" vibratos are just variations on the Strat's design. Rory never got around to using it: his playing was already expressive enough as it was, and the bar would just get in the way.

Dónal Gallagher, Rory's brother and manager, remembers, "The first day he got it, he dispensed with the tremolo arm. I couldn't understand it because we're all huge Shadows fans. Hank Marvin was using the tremolo arm, and to me it's a fantastic feature! [Rory] literally unscrewed it and put it away in a bag. He was playing with the showband and they were doing Shadows numbers, and he knew he could do them without a tremolo."

Rory even blocked the whole vibrato in the back of the guitar with a chunk of wood, turning it into a de facto hardtail. Without the resistance of the springs, it probably helped to keep his bends in tune and arguably helped with the chunkiness of the sound, since more vibrations were transferred from the bridge to the body. Gallagher even developed a visceral aversion to vibrato arms, going as far as breaking off the bars that could not be removed on some of his guitars, like the Corvette and the Kay, leaving a scar that would make most vintage collectors of today go out of their minds. But Rory wasn't a collector per se—he wanted tools and colors, and if a bar got in the way of the tool doing its job, it had to go.

The main stroke of genius with the Strat was its three-pickup configuration. It was probably the main feedback that Leo Fender got from the local musicians who tried out prototypes. Three pickups meant many sounds from just one guitar, from the brightest to the darkest, from the thinnest to the fullest, including the secret "in-between" positions.

Rory would use every possible shade from his Strat, and it was perfectly suited for his every musical need. He could make it sound as big as a Les Paul for chords, thin and biting as a Tele for riffs, or raspy and vocal as a saxophone for his lead work. The three pickups were a big part of it, of course, but it was mostly down to Rory being so familiar with his guitar. That's one of the perks of playing the same instrument for your whole career: you end up knowing exactly where to find what you're looking for, where to pick to get the right sound, how much strength to apply to play the right bend, and how to get to that sweet feedback spot.

At the end of the day, it's almost impossible to tell whether the Strat was a perfect fit for the way guitar playing was evolving in the mid-1960s, or if the guitar itself shaped the evolution of the guitar hero. Before Rory and then Hendrix, few players had the foresight to use the Strat to its full extent, a few notable exceptions being Buddy Guy and Buddy Holly.

When Rory Gallagher bought his Strat in 1963, it was both an obscure instrument and a truly romantic and exotic artifact from the land where the blues was born. It wasn't the omnipresent mass-culture staple we know and love today—at a time when most guitars were traditionally shaped, it took a lot to imagine the possibilities of that double-cutaway instrument. The notion of a solidbody electric guitar wasn't that widespread yet. The Telecaster had only been out for thirteen years when Rory made the jump.

Rory's Strat is rumored to have been the first one to appear on Irish soil, which is impossible to verify but extremely plausible. Its first owner was Jim Conlon, who worked as the guitarist for the Royal Showband, an Irish orchestra that he founded. Like most British guitarists of the time, Conlon was in awe of Hank Marvin's red Strat. Back then, three-color Sunburst was the standard finish, but for a premium you could order a "custom color" from Fender's car-inspired color chart. Marvin's Strat was Fiesta Red, and Conlon wanted the same, but what he got when he ordered it was the 1961 Sunburst. He played it for a few months and when the red one finally arrived, he sold the Sunburst back to the store, where it was priced secondhand at £100. Only fifteen at the time, Rory couldn't even dream of affording it, so he traded in his Rosetti Solid Seven (which probably did not amount to much) and bought the Strat through hire purchase, paying regular installments as the gigs with the Fontana Showband kept coming in.

This is roughly equivalent to £2,200 in today's money (or $3,000), which will get you a nice secondhand Fender Custom Shop guitar—maybe even a Rory Gallagher Relic if you're lucky. Remember, he wasn't buying Rory's Strat; he was Rory buying his Strat! It clearly was more to him than a secondhand guitar: it was a proper made-in-the-USA guitar, an instrument the likes of which few Irishmen had seen at the time except on album covers—if that. The purchase represented a commitment to his trade. He meant business, and that was the instrument that would prove it to the world.

The Sunburst Strat is from a brief era that can be considered the finest version of that

guitar, although every player has their own idea of what a perfect Strat should be. The rosewood fretboard was introduced in 1959, and it went from slab board to veneer board in 1962, basically from a nice chunk of rosewood on the maple neck to a thin strip, which influences both the sound and feel. Those two to three years of production have everything going for them, including the favorable thinner neck and light alder body. Heavier woods would be used after the guitar boom of 1964 to keep up with demand.

Rory wasn't interested in the type of fretboard he was getting, but he knew he wanted a Strat. The following thirty-two years of his career proved him right beyond anybody's expectations, and even though he literally played hundreds of other guitars, not one of them managed to knock the Strat off its pedestal. Unlike many players, Rory never really gelled with more modern instruments, at least not to the point that he would use them as his main stage guitars. Most guitarists, especially at Rory's level, use several guitars for a show, either to get different sounds for different songs, or to remain perfectly in tune while their guitar tech prepares the instruments in the wings. Rory played the Strat for the better part of every single show. It would catch a small break for the acoustic part and a few slide tracks, but the rest of it was all Strat. If it went out of tune Rory would wrangle it back to close-enough-for-rock 'n' roll. This is what in part gave Rory's shows their fiery intensity—no time was wasted changing guitars or getting used to another sound and feel.

Ever-Changing Organism

Rory's Sunburst Strat has a unique beauty to it and it appeared on a lot of album covers through the years: *Deuce* (1971), *Live in Europe* (1972), *Against the Grain* (1975), *Top Priority* (1979), *Stage Struck* (1980), *Jinx* (1982), and *Fresh Evidence*(1990). On *Against the Grain* and *Jinx*, the Strat appears on its own without its owner,

RANGEMASTER
VOX
64351

like a metonymy for Rory himself. The link between the two is so strong that on an album cover, the Strat *is* Rory.

That humanization of the '61 Sunburst Strat is due mostly to its severe wear and tear. In a very Dorian Gray fashion, the Strat bears the marks of every gig and every recording session Rory ever did. It was the definition of a road warrior instrument before that was even a thing. Guitars were not supposed to be that well-worn, and before Stevie Ray Vaughan came along in the 1980s, no one had seen another Strat that showed its scars in such an obvious way. Even Fender execs were miffed that their brand was represented by such a worn-out example. In 1979 they gave Rory a brand-new Strat to replace the '61. Needless to say, that 1979 25th Anniversary model saw little use.

But Rory wasn't beating up his Strat on purpose. In fact, he was quite distressed when it started coming apart, especially after having spent such an enormous amount of money acquiring it. After a show at the Marquee Club in London where he was playing with Taste (which would have been in 1967 or 1968), Rory noticed bits of paint coming off as he was cleaning his guitar. As Dónal Gallagher puts it, "He was actually really upset about that. It was losing the paint. It was never intentional. Nor did he take a hammer, chisel, and a saw, as most people used to think. That's when it really started."

The guitar had already been through a pretty eventful life. In October 1966 it was stolen along with a Telecaster that Rory had borrowed. He contacted the Irish TV Channel RTÉ, which featured the two guitars on a show called *Garda Patrol* to try to locate them. The publicity probably prevented the thief from selling them, so they were dumped in a ditch where they remained for a few days before being retrieved. In the meantime, the Strat was subjected to the hardships of the Irish weather, which is probably when the finish started wearing off, and Rory had been away from his instrument for long enough to realize how precious and truly irreplaceable it was to him. As Dónal tells it, "Rory was in mourning for a week." As Dónal tells it, "Rory was in mourning for a week."

But the element that took away most of the paint away from the instrument arguably was Rory himself: his right-hand strumming was aggressive enough that it actually ended up digging a trench above the pickguard (which clearly shows his favorite picking spot), and he also sweated profusely. He had a particularly acidic sweat caused by a rare blood type, which also affected his liver. Plus, he played long concerts on a de facto lifelong never-ending tour. The website setlist.fm lists 1,900+ shows from 1971 to 1995, an impressive average of more than sixty-eight gigs a year! And that's not counting the 228 shows with Taste from 1967 to 1970 and recording eleven solo studio albums and two Taste studio albums. That's a lot of playing—and a lot of sweating.

Apart from regular refrets with standard Fender wire, the neck was temporarily removed to be dried off, replaced in the meantime by a veneer-board neck. Rory's account of those changes are not so clear, but it seems that the neck was removed a few times over the years.

Rory's sweat was also a threat to the Strat's pickups, but details are somewhat hazy since nobody at the time thought of documenting this aspect of the instrument. Rory regularly tried several pickups on his guitars, and since the Strat was his main instrument, it saw several pickup swaps over the years out of necessity and curiosity. The first known change happened in 1975 when the bridge and neck pickups stopped working at the same time and had to be replaced, presumably with stock Fender pickups of the era, leaving only the original middle pickup. From 1982 to 1984, the bridge pickup had a black cover, but there's no definitive theory on what that black pickup was. Rory went back to a white cover, but there's no saying how many times the pickups were fixed, rewound, or replaced over the course of the Strat's life.

The pickups were examined after Rory's passing, and the final version of the Strat was documented with two Fender pickups in the middle and neck positions (apparently from

the 1970s) and an early DiMarzio FS-1 in the bridge position. It makes sense that, as a relentless tinkerer, Rory would be interested in what Larry DiMarzio was doing, as he was one of the original replacement pickup makers. FS stands for "Fat Strat," which is pretty self-explanatory. That pickup, released in 1974, has a slightly higher output than a regular Fender pickup and more present lows, which would have been a perfect match for Rory's harder-edged music by the end of the 1970s.

As on most Strats of the era, the wiring was "corrected" to include a five-way switch instead of the original three-way, and the middle-pickup Tone knob was turned into a master Tone, leaving the neck-pickup Tone knob unused.

Finally, the Strat is also easily recognizable by its headstock only. The Fender logo has all but faded away, there's an extra string tree on the D and G strings that seems to have been installed in 1974 (the original remains on the B and high E), and the tuners were changed, probably in 1975. Rory might have been trying to get his Strat to remain in tune for a little longer, and he went for the German brand Schaller. The change wasn't convincing to him, so he changed again, this time to the American brand Sperzel. Those Sperzels are vintage models with a split shaft. At some point, the low-E tuner broke and was replaced with a Gotoh tuner that remains today. The five-Sperzels-and-a-Gotoh look remains iconic and perfectly symbolizes Rory's pragmatic and functional approach—so much so that it was even replicated on the Fender Custom Shop version of the guitar.

First-Hand Experience

All these details have made this guitar a true relic in the original religious sense of the term: it is a part of Rory himself, a receptacle for his musical mojo and a dear friend that spent more time with him than most people. Being in the same room as the guitar, especially being able to observe it up close, is incredibly special. It's not unlike seeing the *Mona Lisa* in the Louvre: it's so ubiquitous and it has been represented and replicated so many times that finally getting to experience it in person is a little disappointing at first. Just as the painting is smaller than expected, the guitar is only a great vintage Strat. It takes a few seconds to truly get into the spirit of the object and fully connect with it, to allow yourself to be moved by its presence and aura.

Every detail tells a story, from the holes left by the replaced tuners on the back of the head (next to a missing chunk of wood that begs for an explanation) to the screwdriver spots left around the screws from removing the neck so many times. The serial number is 64351, and the lower twelfth fret dot is pearloid instead of the period-correct "clay." Fender began using pearloid in 1964, so this is another later workaround. But most impressive are the neck, whose back is so dark and dirty it doesn't look like maple anymore, and of course the body, its grayish hue like driftwood on a windy bay, islands of sunburst lost in a sea of bare wood.

Even the case tells a few stories. It's a bulky black molded case typical of the late 1970s and 1980s, not original by any stretch of the imagination. Fenders sold in Europe in the 1960s rarely came with the American case since Fender charged a premium for them. Owners usually opted for local ones. Pieces of tape identify its inhabitant as "Stage Strat," which is both a beautiful understatement and a perfectly fitting potential nickname, and identify its owner as "R.G."—which is all you need to know, really. There are also stickers that attest to a few trips—"AER Lingus FRAGILE" and "British Airways FRAGILE"—but it seems like the days of that case flying as check-in baggage are definitely over.

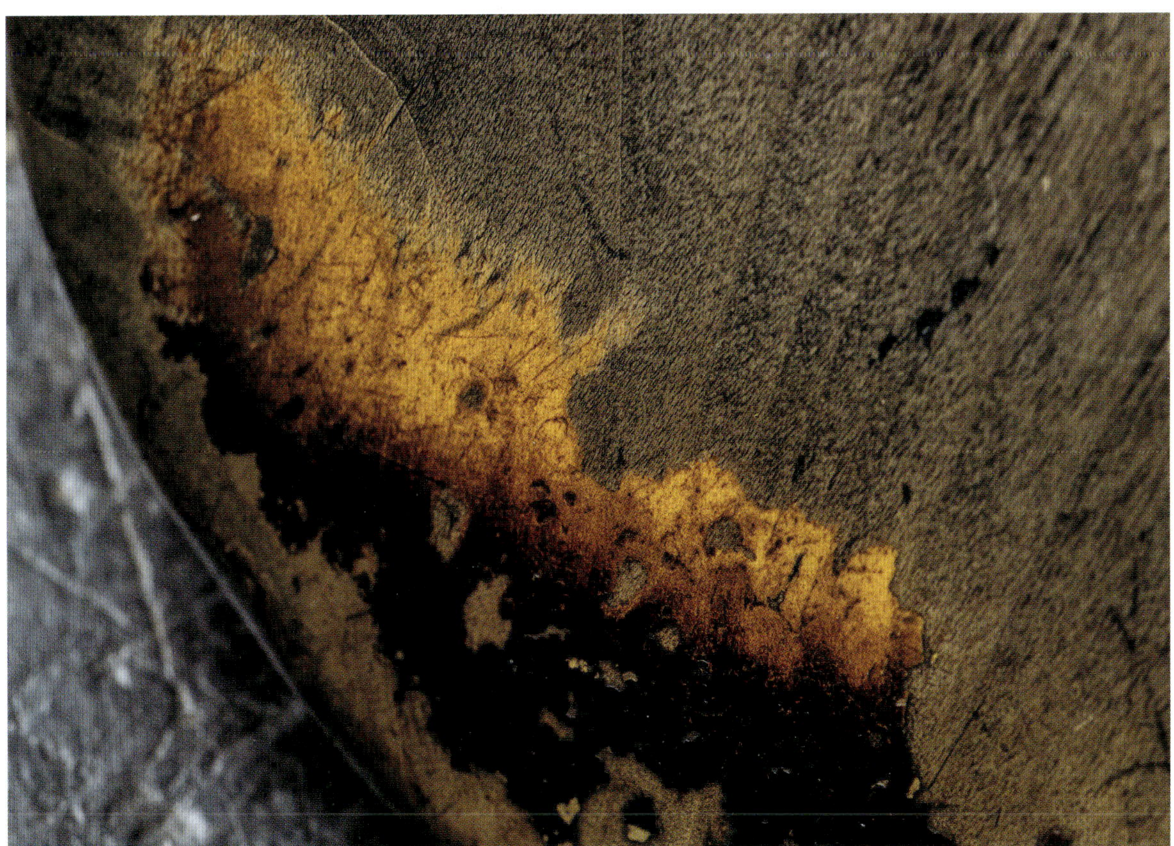

Defining One's Taste

RANGEMASTER
BOOSTER
BOOST
VOX

HIGH POWER
SUPER EFFICIENT
THE
CRESCENDO
ANISOTROPIC
FERRITE
MAGNET

Once the '61 Strat came into the picture, Rory had to find the right partner for his treasured possession at the other end of the cable. His choice of amp was not as plethoric as we are used to by today's standard—and that's putting it mildly—but he still managed to find his own twist on a tried-and-true preference.

British musicians of the early 1960s had access to few locally made amps. Fender tweeds were distant objects of desire that some lucky blokes managed to smuggle in, but given the import tax on goods from the US, they were way too expensive on Rory's side of the pond. Guitar stores and distributors were building and selling their own models at the time, and a lot of them had set shops on Charing Cross Road and Denmark Street next to the offices of music publishers (the area became known as "Britain's Tin Pan Alley"). These shops were at the epicenter of London's burgeoning blues scene, only a few minutes' walk from a hallowed place like the Marquee Club, and included Selmer (a French brand turned into one of the main British gear distributors), Sound City (which belonged to distributor Dallas Arbiter), and Jennings.

Introducing the Top Boost

Jennings started right after World War II in Kent, Dartford, as the Jennings Organ Company, since Thomas Jennings mostly specialized in electric organs. In 1956, he met with big-band guitarist and inventor Dick Denney, who showed him his amp prototype. Jennings was impressed enough that he changed the name of his company to Jennings Musical Industries, even though their line of amps ended up being released under the brand name Vox (Latin for "voice") as early as 1958. The 15-watt Vox AC15 evolved into the AC30—an AC15 with double the power tubes and two speakers—when Hank Marvin requested a more powerful amp from Jennings in 1959. Marvin was playing in the Shadows as Cliff Richard's backing band, and his need for a more powerful tool is a very telling sign of a time when the seeds of rock 'n' roll music were just being planted in the UK.

The Vox AC30 got its legendary look, complete with diamond grille cloth, in 1960. The next evolution was the addition of the Top Boost circuit in 1962. As the name implies, that retrofitting module was a treble booster to help counter the loss of high frequencies resulting from the curly cords and weak pickups of the era. It also added a preamp tube to the circuit, which created a hotter signal that sent the amp into an earlier and warmer distortion. The Top Boost proved so popular that it became a default feature on Vox amps starting in 1963, which ushered in the era of the AC30TB. In the wake of the Shadows, most UK beat and blues bands of the era had a soft spot for Vox, including the Beatles (to this day the British brand's most prominent ambassadors), the Rolling Stones, the Kinks, the Who, the Yardbirds . . . and Rory Gallagher.

Fronting the Fontana

When Rory first discovered the AC30 in 1963, the only available amps were from the first era of British amplification—no Hiwatt, no Sound City, no Laney, no Orange (Marshall was just getting started). The main British brands of the era were Vox, Selmer, and Watkins, with the latter perceived as a cheaper brand. In fact, in 1964, Charlie Watkins changed his brand from Watkins to WEM (Watkins Electric Music) to imitate the three-letter look of the Vox amps. That's how desirable, fashionable, and ubiquitous Vox was at the time.

When Rory bought his AC30, he was buying the other half of his professional-grade gear, the other side of his commitment to a life as a guitar player. He needed an amp that was just as reliable, roadworthy, and great-sounding as his Strat, and in the UK in 1963, the AC30 was the only amp that ticked all those boxes—a true no-brainer. And of course, Hank Marvin's endorsement of the model didn't hurt, since Marvin was among the players who influenced Rory and most of the 1960s British blues scene.

When he joined the Fontana Showband in 1963, Rory borrowed the bass player's AC30 before buying his own. Rory's brilliant and exuberant playing quickly became the main attraction of the act, which he had transformed into the Impact by 1965. Then, Rory struck out on his own in 1966, opting for the power trio formula as the Taste, with Cork musicians Eric Kitteringham (bass) and Norman Damery (drums). The band's name was shortened to Taste, and it became the template for most of Rory Gallagher's future musical endeavors. Taste was, first and foremost, a platform to support and showcase Rory's stunning talents. There was no question as to the leader of the band, all the more so when Gallagher completely changed the lineup in 1968, bringing in Richard McCracken (bass) and John Wilson (drums). Rory was the singer, guitarist, and songwriter in Taste, and the power trio formula was perfect for leaving him enough room to stretch without competition from other soloists, as well as a way to combine spontaneous improvisations with the manageability of a lighter lineup. The formula started to get some traction. Eric Clapton had just put Cream together, and Taste and Cream were highly influential on Jimi Hendrix when he decided that his British band, the Experience, should be a trio as well.

The first version of Taste has not been properly documented on tape (their eponymous debut album was recorded in 1968, after the lineup change), but it deserves its place in rock history as the band that put Gallagher on the map thanks to countless gigs in Ireland. That training period helped Rory define his style and sound so that when he played his residency at the Marquee Club in London in spring 1968, he was fully ready to blow minds.

Mastering the Range

By 1968, the music scene had turned into a very different animal from when Rory had gotten his start back in 1963. Amps and stages had become bigger, Marshall stacks were all the rage, and psychedelia was the name of the game. Rory managed to fit into that scene by remaining true to himself. His music was so pure in its blues essence that it could easily be molded into the listeners' taste of the day—a lesson that would prove extremely precious time and time again throughout Rory's career. In fact, in 1970, when reviewing Taste's second album, *On the Boards*, famed critic Lester Bangs called it "progressive blues," an interesting proposition to say the least.

Rory Gallagher found the missing part of his rig as he was finessing the sound of Taste: the Dallas Arbiter Rangemaster Treble Booster. That gray folded-metal box was one of the early effects units designed specifically for guitarists, along with the early fuzz boxes and tape echoes by Maestro and WEM. Dallas Musical was a London company from Shoreditch that built cheap guitars under several names, but in 1965 they bought the Arbiter company (yet another store), hence Dallas Arbiter, the same brand that released the famous Fuzz Face pedal in 1966.

The Rangemaster was not a booster as we know them today, most of them being units designed to increase volume without drastically affecting sonic character. The Rangemaster was a "treble booster," meaning it mostly affected the upper end of the sonic spectrum, and did so in a particular and recognizable way, courtesy of its sole germanium transistor. In spite of its extremely simple circuit, the Rangemaster could muster fat, sustaining distortion from any amp and turn a woolly crunch into a searing, almost vocal-like affair. In fact, its effect was so drastic that it was not meant to be turned off—it perched on top of your amp with a hardwired output jack and only a small on/off switch next to the Volume control. There was no need for a footswitch; players of the day managed to go from rhythm to lead with the Volume knob on their instrument, a lost art that Rory mastered to a T.

The Rangemaster was just what Rory needed to take the Strat-and-AC30 combo to the next level, from the subtlety of the Fontana Showband to the "progressive blues" of Taste and beyond. The unit could make his Strat sound as fat as a Les Paul and fill just as much sonic space, while keeping the unique brightness of the Vox and the typical Fender clarity, a true secret weapon that did not stay secret for long—Brian May started using the exact same booster and amp after seeing Rory live.

Gearing Up

Rory would treat his Strat as his unequivocal main instrument, but there was no such romanticism attached to the Vox or Rangemaster. There was no particular amp or booster that he would call his number-one rig, and just about any iteration of that combination was all he needed to get his sound. In fact, the two AC30s sold during the 2024 auction sale at Bonhams had been bought in 1970 from the Sound City store in London. Both were pretty beat-up and showed signs of extensive stage use, even though they were not the first AC30s to enter Rory's world. In fact, since they had both been purchased in 1970, they probably came into the picture as backups or replacements for Rory's first AC30.

Interestingly, one of them had markings on the control panel that revealed Rory's preferred settings. The Vib/Trem and Normal channel volumes were set a little past halfway, the Brilliant channel volume was turned all the way down (a clear indication that he was not using that channel at all), and the EQ settings were particularly drastic, with the Treble turned way down (around ten percent), Bass turned all the way up, and Cut turned three-quarters of the way up. Those settings clearly indicate that, even though he was using the none-more-trebly combination of a Strat, a Treble Booster, and a Top Boost–equipped Vox AC30, Rory Gallagher was not looking for an aggressive or shrill sound. The EQ settings and his use of the Normal channel were his way of counteracting the extra treble coming from the Rangemaster while still retaining plenty of bite when he needed it.

In fact, that combo worked so well that it not only defined the sound of Taste and Rory's early solo career, it's also a sound that he revisited to balance the crushing lows of the Marshalls he would use more than a decade later. To this day, in the eyes and ears of fans and guitar geeks, it remains the ultimate "Rory sound."

Looking for Extra Colors

Bjärton Acoustic
Antique Italian Mandolin
1959 Guyatone LG-60B

TILLVERKARE
Bjärton
BJÄRNUM — SWEDEN

The '61 Strat was front and center in Rory's gear for the rest of his career. Yet, as a creative musician who was constantly recording and releasing albums, he was happy to find new colors that would inspire a song, or at least a riff. Those colors didn't need to come from expensive instruments—they could be inspired by a cheap mandolin, a pedal (especially in the 1980s), or a Swedish acoustic bought for the lowly price of £4 on Denmark Street, London.

Bjärton Acoustic

Even though Rory's first guitar was an acoustic, it was more out of necessity and availability than by choice. His strongest musical love was the electric blues, and the Strat was his ultimate tool. But he had a deep acoustic side as well, and he wanted to make that obvious from the get-go. So when Taste entered the De Lane Lea Studios in August 1968 to record the trio's first album, he made sure to include a solo acoustic track. "Hail" is miles from the blistering electric psychedelia featured on the rest of the album, and it remains a unique piece in Rory's discography.

He put the Bjärton guitar bought the year prior to good use with an unusual open tuning: E–A–C#–E–A–E, from low to high. This makes more sense as a strange inverted version of the classic open A tuning, E–A–E–A–C#–E. The C# is much lower than usual, and the second- and third-highest strings have a lower tension than usual. Rory used those quirks to his advantage, exploring notes that could become dissonant in less capable hands. As "Hail" clearly shows, lightning can also strike on a Sweden-made acoustic.

The Bjärton had probably not yet suffered its headstock crack (Rory never mentioned it in an interview), yet it is abundantly clear by looking at the guitar today that the headstock snapped at some point and was reglued in a highly visible way.

Channeling Blind Blake

The Bjärton's short scale gave it a slight buzz with a mostly lowered tuning like Rory's unusual version of open A. These guitars were manufactured in the city of Bjärnum, in the south of Sweden, hence the name Bjärton, literally "the sound of Bjärnum." The company started in 1946, building upright basses, and got into the guitar business in 1952, mostly building archtop guitars. When the skiffle and rock 'n' roll craze hit Europe in the early 1960s, they became much bigger. US-made instruments were extremely scarce and expensive, so European builders like Hagström and Bjärton were the cheaper alternatives that most baby boomers started out with. These were not bad instruments by any means, just thinner-sounding alternatives to the US legends.

Rory's Bjärton has a smaller parlor-size body, not unlike a Martin 00, and a twelve-fret neck with a large V profile typical of American acoustic guitars from the 1920s. This is probably why Rory has been quoted as saying, "Blind Blake used one," even though Blind Blake had been dead for eighteen years when the first Bjärton guitar rolled off the production line. Rory probably actually said something to the effect of "Blind Blake used one like that," which the journalist then transcribed incorrectly. Indeed, in the only known photo of Blind Blake, he's playing a parlor-size acoustic with a twelve-fret neck.

Antique Italian Mandolin

Rory was a master musician, and his craft ran deep. He played the electric and acoustic guitar like nobody's business, but he also played slide on a resonator, he sang, he played the harmonica, he was very adept on the saxophone (as can be heard on "It's Happened Before, It'll Happen Again" off Taste's second album), and he played the mandolin. Rory was not necessarily a virtuoso on the mandolin in the way Bill Monroe was, and it was not a popular instrument in the 1960s, especially with blues players. But the mandolin was close to his heart, probably due to its connections with traditional Irish music.

Rory owned several mandolins over the years, including two Italian-made models. First, he had a round-bodied instrument that met its untimely demise in the early 1970s while Rory was touring the US. The heat was such that the glued-in neck folded on itself. Rory didn't take the time to have it repaired and instead bought this thinner-bodied model.

He found it in a shop in Victoria, London, in 1971. It was built by a luthier named Nicola Naccia in Naples, which is hardly surprising since this city in the south of Italy is famous as the mandolin capital of the world. This specific type of round-back mandolin is even called a "Neapolitan mandolin." But that didn't stop Rory from playing his special blend of Celtic blues on it.

1959 Guyatone LG-60B

As soon as the electric guitar market started to develop in the mid-1950s, many manufacturers tried to get their share of the pie by building cheaper instruments. First, they were built in the US by brands like Harmony and Danelectro. But over time Japanese factories became the *de facto* worldwide suppliers of cheaper electric guitars, due to cheaper labor and an aggressive export policy. When beginners graduated to better guitars, they would sell their Japanese contraptions for dirt cheap at their local pawnshop or music store.

There was a time when any pawnshop in America would be a treasure trove of cheap Japanese guitars. These pawnshop prizes, as they came to be known, weren't necessarily poorly made copies of American brands. Some had their own vibe, their own quirky look, and a sound to match. Most sounded "clearer" than US-made guitars, with more treble and less bass, and the pickups would tend to be very microphonic. Those personality traits could be a disaster in the wrong hands, but they could also inspire something different to an experienced player who needed to be pushed out of their comfort zone. A lot of these guitars ended up being played as slide guitars, since their necks usually

TONE
S
W

had a pretty high action and the slide would eliminate any potential tuning issues. Rory enjoyed pawnshop guitars and he owned a lot of them. While on tour in the US, he would regularly visit smaller stores and pick up a few instruments. Before he got his white Telecaster, he even used a Guyatone as his main slide guitar.

Guyatone is one of the oldest music brands in Japan, founded in 1933. They started off building Hawaiian-style guitars, which were all the rage at the time. They launched their first solidbody electric guitar models in 1955, which were sold in Europe and the US under various names.

The LG-60B was an early model and a higher-end guitar in the Guyatone catalog: there was the 40, the 50, the 60, and the 120, each with different pickups and a different look. The LG-60B had two funny-looking single-coil pickups, with a golden part and a black plastic part with the words "Guyatone Sound Product." They sound extremely clear and trebly, as could be expected.

The model originally came with a bridge cover not unlike the ashtray bridge cover of a Telecaster, but Rory's is missing the cover. Maybe the guitar had already lost it when he bought it. The LG-60B existed with both a three-per-side and six-in-line headstock depending on who was distributing the guitar, in which country, and under which brand.

Even though this particular Guyatone did not see much musical action, the brand would become an important part of Rory's gear history.

Slide of Hand

1966 Fender Telecaster

Fender Twin-Amp

FENDER
PAT.NO.
DES.164227
2,573,254

Once Rory Gallagher had found his undisputed number-one instrument with the '61 Strat, he started his quest for the ultimate slide instrument. Indeed, as a Muddy Waters fan, Rory had a strong penchant for slide playing, and he was no slouch at it either. It can be argued that the blues roots of his playing were never more obvious than when he played with a bottleneck. The use of an alternate tuning would lead him to other sonic destinations than his Celtic-infused pentatonic sound, with a choice of notes that wildly differed from when he played the Strat.

Rory played slide in the open tuning of G (low to high: D-G-D-G-B-D), just like Muddy Waters on his early recordings. This is the "Can't Be Satisfied" tuning, and many other musicians picked up on it, such as Ry Cooder, Keith Richards, and Johnny Winter. Gallagher used a brass slide on his ring finger before moving to a steel slide on his pinky, especially on acoustic guitar where he had to fill more space on his own and appreciated the extra chording possibilities afforded by having his ring finger available. As a side note, Rory got to play with his idol on the 1972 album *The London Muddy Waters Sessions*, alongside a selection of British musicians.

Perfect Slide Instrument

Back when Taste was starting to get some traction, Rory was looking for a guitar that would allow him to express his slide voice. Detuning and retuning the Strat on stage would have been highly inconvenient, and pawnshop guitars like his Guyatone were not the reliable tools he needed. The idea of the Telecaster was planted when he borrowed one from a friend in 1966, as Dónal Gallagher explains:

When he first started Taste in October '66, one of the earliest gigs after Cork was Dublin. It was the big city where you had to prove yourself. A good friend in Cork who had a Telecaster said, "Rory, take my Telecaster up there with you, 'cause what if you break a string?" Rory said, "Nah, I'll be fine," 'cause he could actually change a string while playing from being in the dance bands. But he borrowed it because he loved the sharpness of the Telecaster. On that night in Dublin, they went to visit a journalist for half an hour, and while they were gone the van was broken into. He lost the Strat and his friend's Telecaster. Rory was in mourning for a week. I'd never seen him like that, the depression surrounding him. . . . He was grieving. Fortunately, he had the guitar back after a week. In the meantime, he was using a black Burns guitar.

That misadventure allowed Rory to realize just how much the Strat meant to him, but that was also his first gig with a Telecaster, and something about the brightness of the instrument must have spoken to him. The Tele makes perfect sense as a slide instrument since its high mids nicely cut through the mix and drive the player to use the ample dynamic range allowed by that technique. It is also an extremely sturdy and bare-bones instrument, almost crude when compared with the Strat, but perfect for an open-tuned guitar. It will endure a different tuning without too much fussing with the setup, but it will also gracefully accept its place as a guitar that's only played for two or three songs a night, without the need for new strings before every gig.

From Blonde to White

There was also something about the Tele's pickup configuration that Rory really enjoyed. The second (or "modern") version of the Telecaster's three-position switch wiring gives access to the two pickups in parallel, a sound that was not available on the Strat at that time.

Fender
"TELECASTER"
PAT. 2,573,254

Before the shift to a five-position switch, to get the Strat's famous out-of-phase sounds, you had to lock its switch between two positions with a matchstick, while the Tele already had that sonic option at one's disposal.

Other evolutions of the Tele over the years have been its logo and bridge. As a 1966 model, Rory's white Tele has the "transition" logo, which got its name because it arrived in 1965 when CBS bought Fender, but was ultimately replaced by the "proper" big black CBS version of the logo in 1967. Part of the logo on Rory's Tele had faded, but it is still recognizable. As far as the bridge is concerned, the white Tele originally had threaded steel saddles, which appeared in 1958 on the production model and were replaced with plain steel saddles in 1968. Rory eventually installed those later-style plain steel saddles and he seemed to really enjoy them since he would also use them on his black Esquire.

Feeding Back at the Isle of Wight

The white Tele's main claim to fame is the Isle of Wight concert. Taste was on the festival bill on August 28, 1970, the same day as Tony Joe White, Chicago, Procol Harum, and Cactus. The trio was on the verge of imploding and had only a few months left, but their performance was a pure moment of grace, a swan song of sorts for a cruelly underrated band. Luckily, that show was recorded and filmed. By the time a truncated version of the show was released in December 1971 as *Live at the Isle of Wight*, Taste was long gone and Rory had already released two studio solo albums. Among the songs that were picked for the original version of the live album, "Sinner Boy" stands out and is one of two songs played on the white Tele for that show, along with

N's REC
25 Melros
653-81

"Gambling Blues." It stands out so much, in fact, that it was included in the documentary film about the Isle of Wight festival, *Message to Love*, alongside performances by Jimi Hendrix, Joni Mitchell, and The Who.

Rory's Tele sounds gorgeous on "Sinner Boy," with that typical neck-pickup roundness to the attack. The stage is rather small and the volume must have been deafening, so the Tele feeds back a lot, but never in an ugly or unwelcome way. Rory knows his instrument and he can tame its unpredictable mood.

Even though the "Sinner Boy" sound had an air of perfection to it, Rory was always trying to turn his instruments into their absolute best version. He loved the bite and sting of the bridge pickup, even though he could not control its microphonic tendencies—which may be why he used the neck pickup for the Isle of Wight performance. In the 1980s, he asked his luthier, Chris Eccleshall, to remove the baseplate of the bridge pickup and dip it in wax to avoid any feedback issues. The neck pickup was always problematic: he found it too feeble and muddy compared with the brashness of the bridge, which is why he removed its cover in 1974 to try to get more treble out of it. But the mod's effect wasn't as obvious as Rory had hoped, so the cover was placed back on, which is how the guitar appears in the legendary *Irish Tour '74* movie. The white Tele is front and center on the two electric open-tuning slide songs from that electrifying set, "Who's That Coming" and "Bullfrog Blues," with a cutting sound miles away from the Strat's warm voice.

Rory also experimented with turning the white Tele into a three-pickup instrument in 1979. He installed two extra blade pickups (middle and neck) made by a Nashville musician named Bill Lawrence, who had previously worked with Dan Armstrong and Gibson. His L-220 was a noise-free pickup with a big warm sound courtesy of a higher output level than what is usually expected of a Tele pickup. That three-pickup Strat-like setup on a Tele is usually called a Nashville Tele, but it didn't seem to work for Rory, who switched the white Tele back to its original-ish specs in the late 1980s.

The white Tele may not have been used during every period of Rory's career, but it was one of his main instruments and was the third most expensive electric sold at the 2024 auction. It also was the guitar placed in Rory's hands for his statue outside Belfast's Ulster Hall. The statue, unveiled in January 2025, was based on the front cover of *Melody Maker* magazine, January 1972, featuring Rory playing the Ulster Hall during The Troubles.

1971–1977

The Early Solo Years

Life
On the
Road

1959 Fender Esquire

Fender Twin-Amp

As the Taste adventure came to an end, Rory was fully ready to come into his own as a solo artist. The trio had already gone from complete unknowns to opening for Cream at their Royal Albert Hall farewell concert (November 26, 1968), and they also tagged along for Clapton's next project, opening for Blind Faith on the sole US tour of that short-lived project, in July and August 1969. In 1970, Taste was falling apart at the seams: management issues were turning musicians against each other, and bassist Charlie McCracken and drummer John Wilson wanted to go in a more jazz-oriented musical direction. That was very much part of the zeitgeist at the time, as Miles Davis had just released the seminal one-two punch of *In a Silent Way* (1969) and *Bitches Brew* (1970), creating jazz-rock fusion in the process. McCracken and Wilson ended up joining forces with the ex-guitarist for the Animals and Family, John Weider and ex Blossom Toes member Jim Cregan, with whom they formed the band Stud. In typical jazz-rock fashion, their first album included two tracks that both ran over ten minutes.

The Right Choice

Taste was presented as a band, but it was really a vessel for Rory's creative talent, and he could just as well do it under his own name. In fact, his early solo albums are virtually indistinguishable from the artistic vision of the late Taste. Rory chose to keep the power trio formula, as it allowed him the freedom and the sonic wavelength to stretch his musical feet. His rhythm section came from the band Deep Joy, out of Belfast in Northern Ireland. Bass player Gerry McAvoy had joined Deep Joy back when Brendan O'Neill was still playing drums for the band (he would later play with Rory as well), but by the time Deep Joy was opening for Taste in 1970, Wilgar Campbell had already stepped in. McAvoy's and Campbell's talents did not go unnoticed, since Rory remembered them when Taste imploded and he found himself in need of a solid rhythm section. As luck would have it, Deep Joy had also disbanded by that point, and the two units came together in quite a serendipitous way.

Rory needed a manager, but he had grown wary of a "proper" pro after finding himself tangled in legal issues with his previous manager Eddie Kennedy. This is why he turned down an offer from Peter Grant, who had been managing the Yardbirds since 1966 and was getting Jimmy Page's next project underway. Grant went on to become a legend as the tough-guy Led Zeppelin manager, and the idea of him managing Rory's career remains a big "what if" in the history of rock. Would Rory be even more of a household name if he had signed that deal? Maybe Grant would have pushed Rory to take the Rolling Stones gig in 1975 (more on that later) and the face of the rock world would be different for it. But Rory decided to keep it in the family and his younger brother Dónal became his manager for the rest of his life. Dónal was only one year younger so the two were extremely close, which must have been a comfort for Rory, who spent much of his life on the road. Dónal was his confidant, emotional support, and lifelong friend through the hardships of the music business.

Capturing Lightning

Rory was extremely prolific in the 1970s. His solo albums were released at an impressive pace, starting with his self-titled debut in May 1971, the "Laundromat" album. He chose to produce it himself, with the sole help of sound engineer Eddy Offord, who had previously worked on the second Taste album and was also working with Yes and Emerson, Lake & Palmer at the same time. The album has some great songs and performances, but it possibly missed the fire and passion that would go on to define Rory's live shows. Rory tried to conjure the magic of the live shows with *Deuce*, released in November of the same year, by placing recording sessions closer to shows in the band's schedule.

Then came *Live in Europe* in 1972, recorded only two months before its release. It displays the power of Rory's trio with longer songs that grow on the listener without the need to drive their point across right away. The album was Rory's first major success and gold record, as well as the ultimate proof that his music should be experienced up-close.

In order to keep up with his punishing touring schedule (about 100 shows in 1971, 116 in 1972, and 181 in 1973), Rory needed proper tools that he could rely on. There was no question that his 1961 Stratocaster would be the main instrument for every show he played, and his arsenal was beginning to grow with the addition of the white Telecaster for slide work and his Martin D-35 for acoustic parts. Rory was always looking for more guitars, as tools for inspiration or just beautiful artifacts of Americana. The fact that he was regularly

touring in the US was extremely helpful in that quest, since most of the great guitars had been made there and were available in pawnshops and guitar stores.

But sometimes the guitars found Rory without him having to look for them. That is how he became the owner of his 1959 Esquire in 1971. Its previous owner cold-called Rory and told him he had an interesting guitar, which he misidentified as a 1953 model. The confusion is easy to understand, as information about vintage guitars wasn't widespread or even readily available at the time. In fact, the very idea of a "vintage" guitar wasn't even a notion. They were secondhand instruments and players in the know were just starting to understand that maybe the older ones were better than the new ones.

But Esquires didn't change much over the course of the 1950s, which makes it really hard to date one without taking it apart. Rory's guitar first appeared in his collection with a black pickguard, a modification that was probably done prior to him buying the guitar to accommodate its extra neck pickup (an Esquire, in original form, is basically a Telecaster with a single bridge pickup and no neck pickup). The guitar's yellowish finish would have been the only tell-tale sign of a late-'50s Esquire. Or rather the *other* tell-tale sign, since Rory's Esquire is equipped with a top-loading bridge. This is a rare feature that only appears on late-1958 and early-1959 Teles and Esquires, a rarity that has never gotten much traction, even from vintage guitar fanatics. The top-loader's strings are strung through the bridge instead of through the body, making it more akin to Gibson's wraparound tailpiece. Top-loading Teles are seen as slightly more responsive with a little less sustain, but that didn't seem to bother Rory. In fact, it might have been a good thing for slide playing.

Rory already had the white Tele, but that blonde Esquire (he would sometimes refer to it as a Tele since it had been modded with a second pickup) soon became his other slide guitar. It can be seen in the Beat Club performance, used for the songs in open E (from low to high: E–B–E–G#–B–E), and even though the colors are close, it is easy to tell apart from the white Tele (which he used for the open G songs), since it is the only guitar with a maple fretboard in Rory's arsenal at that point. For that performance, the Esquire has a black pickguard with drawings representing the sun, the moon, and what look like Native American teepees. This could have been of Rory's making, since the American Wild West was an endless source of fascination for the Irishman, including in some of his lyrics like "Out on the Western Plain."

Through Hell and Black

After that first sighting, the Esquire had a complicated life, and it can be hard to pinpoint exactly when its many mods were undertaken. For reliability's sake, Rory changed the tuners as soon as he got the guitar, but then a terrible accident happened. Dónal Gallagher recalls:

Much to Rory's horror, the Tele suffered a terrible thrashing at an airport. We actually watched it happen, it was like slow motion for us. The guy with one of these tractors taking the baggage off the plane, the guitar falling off the conveyor belt coming out of the aircraft, and the guy driving over the case and the guitar. We were inside this small airport somewhere in Michigan looking outside and we knew it was gonna happen. The guitar was so badly scraped. Instead of going to the hotel like we normally would, he went straight to the gig and plugged it into an amp to see if it worked. And it did! You can't kill a Telecaster, it's a beast of an instrument. When we finished the American tour, we got back to Chris Eccleshall for repair, to rebuild the damaged parts. After a couple of weeks, I went to collect it and brought it back to Rory. When he opened the case, he went, "Oh no, he's destroyed it! He's sprayed it green." From the original cream, the guy sprayed it green, thinking—very English of him—Rory being from Ireland, he would appreciate the color green.

Other accounts place the infamous airport incident after a tour, in which case there would have been no "going straight to the gig." And according to Eccleshall himself (who was Rory's guitar tech at the time), the green hue was not intentional but a result of not having enough time to work on the guitar between two tours and leaving the lacquer to only partially dry. One thing is certain: in 1972, the Esquire was crushed but it survived. The break in the wood being cleaner than it might have been, Eccleshall managed to put it back together. At this point the Esquire got its plain-groove saddles, just like those on the white Tele, and a white pickguard, like it originally would have had when it was built in 1959.

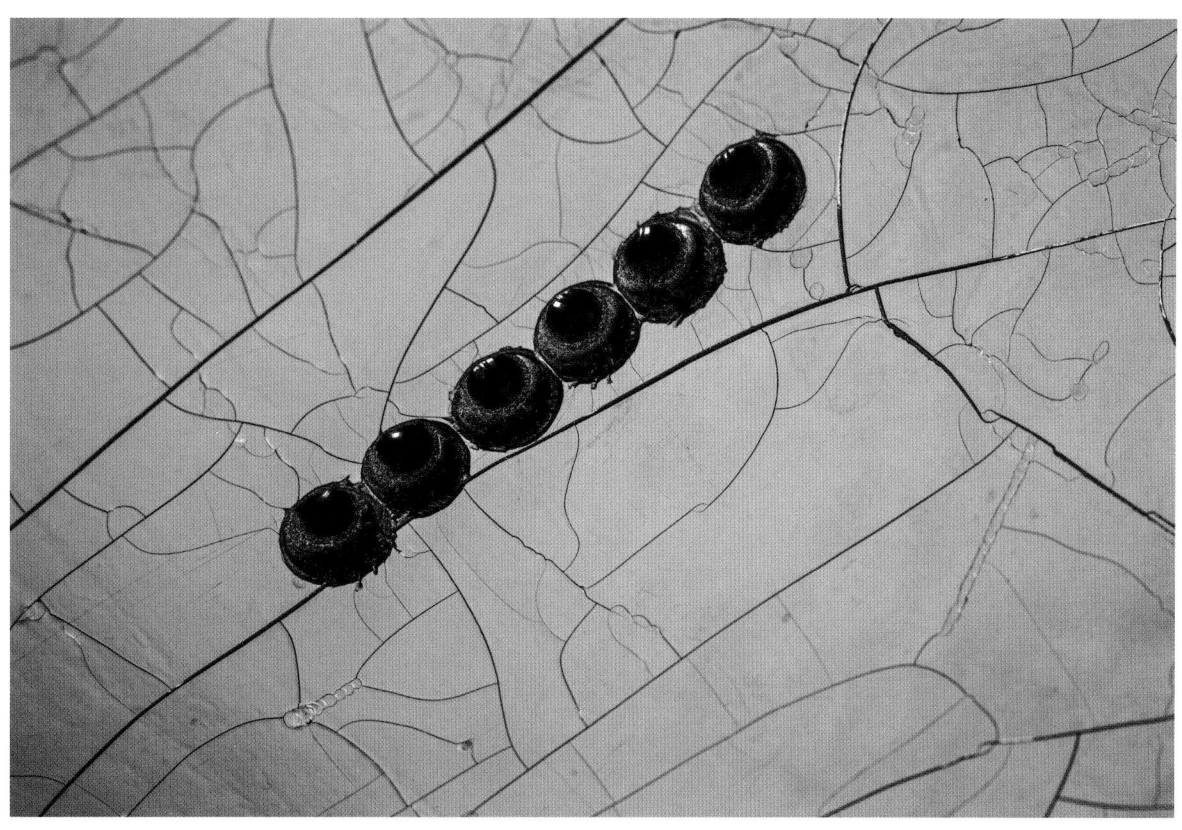

FENDER
PAT. NO.

After that, Rory used the guitar for recording the *Blueprint* album (1973), at which point it appeared to have its fretboard sanded off, either to give it a flatter radius, to remove grime, or for a simple refret. The newer frets were bigger and Rory seemed to favor jumbo or at least larger frets on most of his guitars, including Fenders. A second refinish by Eccleshall at the end of 1972 turned it into the black Esquire that it is today, which explains the checking that doesn't really look like an original Fender finish would look after years of playing. The lines are too wide, and they draw a picture that's all too clear, especially on the bottom in the front.

The last modifications were akin to what Rory did to his white Tele: he started by removing the cover of the neck pickup in 1975, then replaced it altogether with a Strat pickup since he wasn't satisfied with his previous try. Then he added a switch between the Volume and Tone controls that allowed him to put the two pickups out of phase with each other, giving it a special quacky sound not unlike positions 2 and 4 of a Strat. In 1976, Rory turned the Esquire into a "Nashville Tele," that is, adding a third (Strat) pickup in the middle position and installing a five-way switch in place of the original three-way to accommodate the mod. Then, he removed the extra out-of-phase switch before changing the control plate altogether. He also replaced the failing bridge pickup with a Tele pickup before retiring the guitar from live use in 1978. Through all those changes, the neckplate has remained the same, with the mysterious inscription "Property of Buzz Harding, Greensburg, Kansas."

When the Esquire finally reappeared for the *Defender* album nine years later (especially on the track "Loanshark Blues"), it had been turned into the regular black Tele it is now, featuring two pickups and a back-loading bridge. Not much is left of the Esquire that left the Fullerton factory in 1959, yet it can be argued that guitar probably had the most fun out of its particular batch.

The Acoustic Side

1968 Martin D-35
1930 National Triolian Resonator
Harmony Sovereign H1270
1942 Martin Style A Mandolin

FRAGILE
FRÁGIL
Hannovers
Folk- und Bluesknepipe
OTENKISTE

Even though the immortal image of Rory is him with his '61 Strat, he also was a brilliant acoustic player. His style on the steel strings was less flashy, less loaded with electricity, but no less exciting—far from it. In fact, it might be where his playing had the most range: he could go from solid singer-songwriter country strumming to badass fingerpicking and everything in between, in standard or open tuning, with or without a capo.

1968 Martin D-35

And he did it all with just one guitar: his trusted Martin D-35, which is the acoustic equivalent of his Strat. He played it throughout his career, used it on stage at almost every show, and relied on it at home for songwriting and in the studio for recording. Apparently, the acoustic heard on "I'm Moving On," the closer on Taste's debut album in 1969, is not the Martin. As Dónal Gallagher puts it, "Richard [McCracken], the bass player with Taste, had a couple of guitars; he had a Gibson and a jumbo acoustic that Rory would have to borrow for recordings."

On the Boards (1970) was a decidedly electric affair that cemented Rory's image as a Strat-wielding blues soloist. Only one song really exhibits his acoustic ability, but it's a good one: on "See Here," he's alone and accompanies his singing with a gorgeous fingerpicked part in a strange open tuning: D–A–D–A–D–F#. This unusual approach to traditional D tuning still forms a D major chord with the open strings, but the top three strings are tuned higher than usual. The resulting extra tension gives the Martin a nice bright ring.

Acoustic Landscapes

But the acoustic revelation is the 1971 eponymous solo debut, so much so that it can almost be considered as half electric blues record/half songwriting effort that could have come out of Laurel Canyon during the same era. "Just the Smile" is the second song on the album and a strong Celtic-infused folk song with an understated rhythm section. The driving acoustic rhythm is played with a pick on the Martin tuned to D–A–D–G–A–D, which is arguably the most popular Celtic tuning. It has an extremely recognizable sound from the presence of the fourth (G) among the octaves of D and its fifth, A. British guitarist Davey Graham popularized this tuning, who single-handedly invented the idea of a folk guitar instrumental in 1962 with his hit "Anji," later covered by Paul Simon. The tuning was then used by John Renbourn and Bert Jansch, the two guitarists from the British band Pentangle, and Richard Thompson from Fairport Convention. The three had already started their solo careers by the time Rory's first album was released, and the way they took the British Celtic music heritage to invent their own version of the American folk music popular at the time proved highly influential. In fact, most fingerstyle players of the following generations, from Peppino D'Agostino to Pierre Bensusan and Michael Hedges, chose D–A–D–G–A–D tuning after growing up listening to those players. Even Jimmy Page used it for "Kashmir" a few years after borrowing a Bert Jansch acoustic instrumental for the first Led Zeppelin album ("Black Mountain Side"). It only made sense that Rory identified with the music of Renbourn, Jansch, and Thompson since their Celtic influences would sound quite familiar to an Irishman who grew up surrounded by the music of his land.

But there's more to Rory's acoustic side. Much more. "Wave Myself Goodbye" and "I'm Not Surprised" have a completely different feel, veering toward ragtime. Ragtime originally was a blues piano style in the early 1900s, but guitar players embraced it and adapted it to the guitar. The bass notes from the left hand on the piano are played with the thumb (or a thumb pick) on the two or three low strings, while the melody (the right hand on the piano) is picked with the remaining fingers on the high three to four strings. This technique turns the guitar into a small orchestra without the need for a band, especially with the deep bass notes of the dreadnought-style Martin.

Blind Blake was an early master of the ragtime guitar and a strong influence on Rory's playing. As he died at a young age back in 1934, little is known about him except for the songs he recorded between 1926 and 1932. But his legacy has endured with the help of a few players who were deeply influenced by him, especially Reverend Gary Davies and Big Bill Broonzy, the latter being especially popular with British Invasion artists. Blind Blake's influence on Rory's approach is so strong that many examples of ragtime songs appear in his early discography, including: "Pistol Slapper Blues" on *Live in Europe* (1972), "Unmilitary Two-Step" on *Blueprint* (1973), and "20:20 Vision" on *Tattoo* (1973).

Elsewhere, Rory plays blues slide on his Martin on "Banker's Blues" (*Blueprint*); picks country on "It's You" (first album) and "Tucson, Arizona" (*Tattoo*); strums à la *All Things Must Pass*–era George Harrison on "If I Had a Reason" (*Blueprint*); and dazzles with up-tempo fingerpicking on "Out of My Mind" (*Deuce*). All that on the same Martin D-35.

Uncharted Territory

Rory bought his Martin D-35 secondhand in 1969. It is a 1968 model, still with the Brazilian rosewood back and sides. Martin was switching to East Indian rosewood at the time

because Brazilian was getting harder to track down. In fact, that scarcity is how the model was created in the first place. The D-35 appeared out of pure necessity in 1965, making it a relatively recent introduction compared to the other dreadnought-shaped Martins. Many Brazilian rosewood sets were too small to be used for the two-part back of the classic D-28, so Martin designed the beautiful three-part back of the new D-35. Introduced as a more upscale option, the D-35 was helped by the addition of a neck binding, Grover tuners, and a lighter bracing that gave it a bigger, deeper sound than the D-28, its close sibling.

Unlike the Strat, which Rory chose partly as a Buddy Holly fan, the Martin D-35 was so new that it didn't carry any artistic baggage. The D-28 has been played by Elvis Presley, Johnny Cash, and Hank Williams, to name a few, but the D-35 was uncharted territory that Rory could make his own. He picked it up for the sound, the big blooming bass we expect from Martin's dreadnought shape. The D-35 would become Martin's bestselling model in 1974, and other artists picked it up as their weapon of choice, including David Gilmour, Johnny Cash, and Johnny Marr, the latter in no small part influenced by Rory.

In fact, Rory is now revered as one of the main musicians associated with the D-35, and Martin released a special Rory Gallagher version in 2008. This limited edition of twenty-nine guitars was for the UK market only, a classic D-35 with Rory's signature on the nineteenth and twentieth fret, as well as Dónal's signature on the inside label.

Taking It to the Stage

Unlike Rory's electrics, very few mods were done to the D-35. He changed the bridge as soon as he got it to get proper intonation, which can't be adjusted otherwise on most acoustics. Then, he took the time to play it

until it was good enough by his standards. He told *Melody Maker* in 1975, "The thing about a Martin is that it takes about five years to play itself in, it has to develop through a whole lot of things like the heat of the player's body, the atmosphere it's played in and all that. . . . When I first got the Martin, I've gotta say that I was a bit disappointed, but as I played it, the guitar seemed to get better."

Of course, there's a degree of scientific truth to that. The structure of the wood changes as the guitar gets older and every element has properly dried, and the player's favorite notes and positions resound in a particular way from micro wear. This is one main reason for the popularity of vintage guitars. It is also interesting to note that, even though he was disappointed with the original sound of his D-35, Rory stuck with it and played it into being the instrument he was hoping for. Martins were not that common in Britain at the time, and a player's first Martin was a major step toward the big league. This was the sign that they were serious, basically the symbolic equivalent of the Strat on the electric side. Instead of hunting down another better dreadnought, Rory had music to play and tours to do. He might also have understood that a guitar, especially an acoustic one, adapts to the player, and that while an older one could have been more broken-in, it wouldn't necessarily have fit his approach.

The replaced bridge left some marks around it on the guitar's top, and the pickguard has a few glue stains around it. Although it's impossible to say when, it was replaced at

some point, most likely because the identical original—which remains in the case to this day—had warped slightly, a common problem because plastic tends to shrink over time.

Finally, the Martin also had to be equipped to be used on stage. In the 1960s, acoustic guitars on stage were usually miked with a simple vocal microphone that would generate feedback and also hinder the performer's ability to move around, especially when trying to compete with a band. In the 1970s, several makers started experimenting with piezo pickups to get a strong, clean sound out of their acoustic guitars. Ovation started the trend following a request from Glen Campbell, and the brand became ubiquitous among players who performed to large crowds with an acoustic. But Rory wasn't prepared to switch over to Ovation after years of turning his D-35 into what he wanted it to be, so he installed an aftermarket piezo ceramic contact pickup, the Ibanez 2000, a.k.a., "The Bug." Released by the Japanese brand in 1975, this pickup is a small rectangle with a built-in cable and an RCA connector, requiring an RCA-to-jack adapter that can still be found in the Martin's beat-up hardshell case. Rory plugged into a Barcus Berry 1330 preamp to get proper volume out of the pickup. That solution was spartan by today's standards, and Rory tried newer solutions in the 1980s, but until then it worked for him—so much so that he installed the same Ibanez pickup on his mandolin.

Like the Strat, the D-35 is a central part of Rory's gear, a mainstay throughout the years. Fans could feel it too, and they turned it into the second most expensive guitar sold at the 2024 auction.

CUSTOM BUILT GUITARS
& BASSES
Keith Thompson (0462) 59912
SXB
IT 5401
ORY
EuroClass

1930 National Triolian Resonator

The resonator guitar was still an obscure relic from the past when Rory Gallagher purchased this National Triolian. Few players were using this style of instrument, and even though it has become a classic blues tool in the meantime, the resonator guitar remains a rarity nowadays, both in guitar stores and on stage.

The instrument was invented in the late 1920s by musician George Beauchamp and luthier John Dopyera. As a performer, Beauchamp needed more volume from his instruments to be heard properly. That was the main challenge for guitar designers of the day, and several builders looked for solutions. Martin and the Larson Brothers invented larger-bodied acoustic flat-tops that projected more, while Rickenbacker, Les Paul, and Gibson worked on magnetic pickups to plug the guitar into an amp. But Beauchamp and Dopyera came up with a completely different idea: three metal cones (called resonators) inside a steel body that would make the guitar sound louder and more aggressive.

Together, Dopyera and Beauchamp formed the National company. But then in 1929, Dopyera created a new brand with the help of his brothers, Dobro (short for Dopyera Brothers). Dobros had a simpler single-cone design than National's "tricones," but the resonator idea never really picked up. A few blues and bluegrass players used them for their sharp sound, but generally speaking, it was too heavy and sounded too brash for most play-

ers, especially blues players hoboing around America who couldn't be bothered with such a cumbersome tool. Nowadays, we are used to seeing blues players using resonator guitars, but this is mostly due to them being picked up by Taj Mahal, Mark Knopfler, Johnny Winter, and Rory himself in the 1970s and 1980s. The most famous original Delta blues singers who played resonator instruments were Bukka White, Bo Carter with the Mississippi Sheiks, Blind Boy Fuller, and, most importantly, Son House. The Mississippi-born bluesman was active in the 1930s and had a deep influence on both Robert Johnson and Muddy Waters. He remained mostly unknown until musician Al Wilson (from Canned Heat) found him and encouraged him to take up playing and recording again in the 1960s. As one of the few artists still alive from that era, he became a true inspiration for many students of the blues, including Rory.

Closer to the Heart

Resonator guitars were extremely hard to find in the UK in the 1970s, so Rory seized the opportunity to purchase his while touring the US in spring 1973. A traveling guitar salesman offered it to him for a decent price—$100 dollars as Rory remembers it, or about $750 in today's dollars. It is a relatively simple version of the National guitar, a single-cone Triolian made in 1930. The Triolian was originally a cheaper wood-bodied guitar before it became

a steel model with a Bakelite neck. Rory's is the third version, with a maple neck. The body meets the neck at the twelfth fret, which Rory didn't seem to mind too much, and the original sunburst paint has all but faded to a dark-yellow hue, with the steel showing through in many spots.

As with most of Rory's guitars, the National has been through a few changes. The most obvious is the new fretboard, which looks cleaner than the rest of the instrument. Plus, it has a binding and two dots at the fifteenth frets, both features that were not part of the original National design. The bridge has also been changed, and the resonator was crushed during a plane flight and had to be replaced.

Rory didn't waste any time putting it to good use, and he started including his version of "As the Crow Flies" in his live setlist in August 1973 at the Rainbow Theatre in London. The song had only been released a year prior on Tony Joe White's fifth album, *The Train I'm On*. Even though it was written by White, it became Rory's signature resonator song, especially after the release of the *Irish Tour '74* live album. The song is an absolute standout track on a standout live album, and the deep, biting sound of the National tuned to open D (D–A–D–F#–A–D) is a major part of its charm. At the time, the guitar had already had its fretboard changed.

Rory also used it for several major shows, including a beautiful performance on French TV in 1975 (featuring the National on "All Around Man" and "Too Much Alcohol") and a touching version of "Secret Agent" in 1977 for an Irish TV channel.

Finally, the National made a significant comeback in the studio in 1990, on what would be Rory's final studio album, *Fresh Evidence*. He tuned to open G on the song "Empire State Express," written by none other than Son House. *Fresh Evidence* is a richer-sounding album than most of Rory's studio releases, but "Empire State Express" appears as a stark and deeply honest solo interlude, a true moment of intimate grace that makes it feel like you're sitting in front of Rory, listening to an awe-inspiring performance. The National acted as a true revealer for the simple beauty of Rory's playing.

Harmony Sovereign H1270

Nowadays, twelve-string acoustics are seen mostly as barely playable relics of the chiming 1970s, back when Laurel Canyon singer/songwriters used them to strum along with their tales of woe. Rory Gallagher was not completely removed from that world, as can be heard on "I'm Not Awake Yet," a strange track off *Deuce* (1972) on which the twelve-string acoustic plays along with the Strat.

Before the 1960s, the twelve-string was a bona fide blues instrument, a true boon for solo singers looking for rich-sounding accompaniment. Of course, twelve strings are also a lot to take, even if they're really six courses, that is, six doubled strings, which harkens back to an ancient tradition of multiple-course instruments, like the Egyptian oud and the Mexican bandolón. It takes more finger strength to play a twelve-string guitar, especially with the high action typical of older instruments, so initially only two musicians became synonymous with it: Lead Belly and Blind Willie McTell. Both used the fuller, thicker sound of the twelve strings to play more instrumental parts, and both played Harmony-made jumbo guitars.

Harmony started in the late nineteenth century and became the biggest instrument builder in the US during the 1920s and 1930s. At the time, Harmony belonged to Sears, Roebuck and Co. and the location of its factory in Chicago put it right at the center of all the postal roads. In 1930, Harmony built a half million instruments, including guitars, ukuleles, and mandolins.

The brand then became independent and had another peak at the height of the British Invasion. Among Harmony's bestselling models of the mid-1960s was the Sovereign, which took its name from a brand bought by Harmony in the 1930s. It was the big acoustic of the line: huge body, ladder bracing, and a thick twelve-fret neck and a separate tailpiece to endure the massive tension created by twelve strings. Its six-string counterpart (model 1260) became legendary for being used by Jimmy Page and Pete Townshend, whereas the twelve-string version (model 1270) was favored by Keith Richards and Rory.

Rory used his Harmony a lot, most notably on "Don't Know Where I'm Going" off *Deuce*, where he channels his inner Lead Belly, playing solo with guitar and harmonica. He bought the twelve-string in November 1972 from the London music store Take Five and had to reset the neck in order to tune to regular pitch. The tension on the neck was such that the guitars were designed to be tuned down two steps (Lead Belly tuned down to B and Blind Willie McTell tuned down to C or lower) to make the guitars playable and take stress off the neck. But Rory wanted to play it in standard tuning, so a luthier unglued the neck and put it back at a more favorable angle. The tricky operation was worth it because Rory used the guitar throughout his career.

1942 Martin Style A Mandolin

As previously mentioned in regard to Rory's Italian mandolins, the Irish genius was always drawn to the instrument. Since the mandolin's glory days were long gone by the 1960s, this set Rory apart as a bluesman unafraid to try something different.

This Martin entered Rory's life in the early 1970s and can be heard on "Going to My Hometown" from his first live album, *Live in Europe '72*. The song remained a signature mandolin number throughout Rory's career and was invariably performed on this 1942 Style A, including in the movie *Irish Tour '74*.

The American brand Martin has been making mandolins for almost as long as they've been making guitars, starting in the late 1800s. Rory's love of Martins is consistent with his no-nonsense workingman ethos. A no-frills Martin is the ultimate workhorse, with none of the fancy accoutrements found on other brands (even Martin's higher-end models).

The Style A is among Martin's simplest mandolins, and it bears the Italian influence in its oval soundhole (as opposed to f-holes) and overall shape. The model appeared as early as 1914, and the sides and back were switched from rosewood to mahogany in 1917. The top has always been made of spruce, but in 1937 its standard color went from natural to sunburst, or as Martin called it "Shade Top." The new finish was a more work-intensive color to apply, but the sunburst was also a good way to hide imperfections in the spruce woodgrain that would otherwise require discarding the wood.

Rory's Style A was made in 1942, right before the US entered World War II and production was all but stopped to focus on the wartime effort. When he got the mandolin, he quickly added a second pickguard on the bass side to protect the top from his aggressive pick attack. This explains the obvious difference between the two pickguards, the newer one being smaller and redder than its treble-side counterpart. He also needed to amplify it to use it on stage, so he went for the same solution as his D-35: an Ibanez 2000 pickup. Its cable and RCA output connector were stuck to the side of the mandolin with adhesive putty, a solution that would make most luthiers wince but seems to have done the trick for a good twenty years.

Last, Rory's Style A has a replaced tuner for the fourth string, the second D. It is bigger and whiter than the other seven, like a poetic echo of the mismatched high E tuner on his Strat.

From a Trio to a Quartet

Fender Twin and Fender Bassman and Hawk II Tonal Expander

Fender Twin-Amp

Fender Bassman detail

The year 1972 was a big one for Rory and his trio. The band was riding high after the critical and commercial success of the first live album, and they performed more than a staggering 120 shows this year. It took a toll on drummer Wilgar Campbell, who developed a fear of flying so debilitating that he missed a few shows that year. To avoid canceling the shows, Rory had to find a temporary replacement quickly, which came in the form of bassist Gerry McAvoy's London roommate, Rod de'Ath. The Welsh musician was part of Killing Floor, a London-based blues band who took their name from a Howlin' Wolf song. After a few shows during the summer of 1972, it became apparent that de'Ath was fit for the job. He became a permanent fixture in Rory's band, quickly followed by his ex–Killing Floor bandmate, keyboardist Lou Martin. Like McAvoy, Martin was born in Belfast and a dyed-in-the-wool blues enthusiast.

The band went from a trio to a quartet and didn't waste any time entering the London Marquee Studios in December 1972 to record Rory's fourth album, *Blueprint*. From the opening track, "Walk on Hot Coals," the difference is obvious: the band sounds fuller and more laid-back. Rod de'Ath's drumming is busier and louder than Campbell's, while Lou Martin's electric piano, mixed to the right-hand side, is the perfect complement to Rory's guitar. The interplay between the two is striking, as well as the fact that Rory doesn't need to fill up as much space as he used to. His playing becomes slightly more nuanced, even though his sound seems a little trebly compared with Martin's fatter Wurlitzer.

Fender Twin and Fender Bassman

To adapt to this new sonic context, Rory decided to try a new approach. He stopped using the AC30 and Rangemaster altogether and switched to Fender tweeds. Tweed is a generic nickname for the Fender amps of the 1950s, a nickname earned from their elegant covering. Before that, the first amps made by the then-new company had bare-wood panels (hence their nickname "woody"), and in the early 1960s, Fender switched to cream or brown Tolex (hence blonde or brownface). But it's not just about the looks: those tweed amps had a sound of their own, a spongier feel, a natural compression, and a dirtier, crunchier tone due to the lack of headroom that would be corrected on future amps.

The first Fender tweed to enter Rory's rig in 1973 was a Twin amp, the higher-end and most powerful model of the bunch with two 6L6 tubes producing a whopping 40 watts through two 12-inch speakers (hence the "Twin" name). This is what collectors would later call the "low-powered Twin" to differentiate it from the post-1958 "high-powered twin" with twice as much output power.

But the Twin on its own sounded a little too dark and didn't have the width or dynamic range of the Vox, so Rory quickly added a second tweed amp to build the perfect dynamic duo with the Twin: a 1954 Fender Bassman. When Fender invented the electric bass with the Precision Bass in 1951, they needed an amp to plug it into. It took a few months, but in 1952 they came out with the Bassman. Even though the name doesn't leave much doubt as to its purpose, guitar players quickly adopted the Bassman like Buddy Holly and Buddy Guy (again with those Strat pioneers!), as it offered better headroom and more bass response than other amps. The Bassman was even used as the template for the first Marshall amps. Rory's Bassman was made in 1954, making it one of the first "narrow panel" models, as opposed to the "wide panel" look of the previous version. It features four 10-inch speakers for a width akin to the AC30.

Rory's tweed Fenders were modified and repaired throughout the years. Both had a voltage selector installed to easily switch from 110 volts (US) to 240 volts (UK), and the mismatched speakers on both models seem to indicate that some were replaced. The Bassman also had a front logo replaced. Instead of the script "Fender Bassman," Rory's amp has an earlier all-caps FENDER logo misplaced on the right side of the front panel. As with any tweed amp from that era, the Bassman's covering shows its age in a graceful way.

This page: Fender Twin

This page: Fender Bassman

This page:
Fender Bassman

Hawk II Tonal Expander

Unlike the Twin that could deliver a nice crunch without any outside help, the Bassman needed a little push to really get cooking. The Vox had its Rangemaster, but Rory decided to pair the Bassman with a lesser-known boost unit, the S. Hawk Ltd. Hawk II Tonal Expander. New York amp builder Harry Kolbe designed the unit in 1973, at a time when the very idea of a booster was intrinsically linked with the Rangemaster.

The Hawk II takes a few ideas from the Rangemaster playbook, including its "always on" philosophy, but it also adds many new features. First, it requires two 9-volt batteries instead of one, for a higher output-level resulting in more boost: +20dB of regular boost and +30dB of treble boost. The three controls on top are true large amp-style switches. The red one on the left turns the unit on, but the off position is not just a bypass of the unit, it completely turns off any sound. The middle switch activates the gain boost, while the right switch activates the treble booster. Then, there are the big sliders below that control the three-band EQ, with points specifically designed for the guitar: 170Hz, 550Hz, and 2,500Hz.

Unfortunately, S. Hawk Ltd. never really met public acclaim, and the Tonal Expander was only built for two years. Still, Rory seemed to think of it as the perfect companion to his Bassman, and he used it for a few years to complement Lou Martin's Wurlitzer and Hammond organ sounds.

The Stones Audition

Fender Deluxe

Fender Deluxe
FULLERTON CALIFORNIA

RADIOSPARES

By January 1975, Rory was slowly turning into a household name thanks to the success of *Irish Tour '74*. His contract with Polydor had ended and he was completely free to explore any opportunity. This is when Dónal Gallagher got a phone call in the middle of the night, as he recalled in a 2012 interview with Pierre Journel from *La Chaîne Guitare*.

We had just finished the Irish Tour, we were in our home in Ireland and it was Ian Stewart, the sixth Rolling Stone if you like, the keyboard player and original founding member of the band. He called to know if we were interested to come to Rotterdam and have a jam. Rory agreed, he's a huge Stones fan anyway so he knew the material. It was arranged for mid-January, but then they kept postponing the session. By the end of January, Rory had a tour to do in Japan.

So he went to Rotterdam, Mick Jagger picked him up at the airport. Marshall Chess Jr., the manager of the band, greeted Rory at the door and said, "Welcome to the Rolling Stones, you're the guy for the job!" Rory said, "Hang on, I just came to jam!" The first night, Keith didn't come. He wasn't talking to Mick, they were not communicating, so Rory was in a difficult position. The first night, Mick had written a song and he wanted a riff, so they worked on a song with Charlie on the drums. The sessions would start around midnight. Keith came down the next day for the evening sessions, Rory would spend the rest of the day talking to Bill and Charlie. It was going very well, so on the last evening, Rory said to Mick, "What's going on, I'm supposed to be flying to Tokyo from London tomorrow." And Mick said, "We'd like you to stay, can you go and speak to Keith?" So Rory went to Keith's bedroom and Keith was comatose. Rory stayed through the night and kept trying to wake Keith. He finally gave up and went back to London then straight to Tokyo. But trying to communicate with someone in Tokyo at the time was complicated. The Stones called the agent in London who told them Rory wasn't interested, we only found that out afterwards. That wasn't the case, Rory was just very confused as to what the Stones exactly wanted from him, they kept changing the arrangements. Rory, being the kind of guy he was, wouldn't cancel the Japanese tour. Also I think he wanted to demonstrate that he was his own guy, that he didn't want to be just a sideman. He deserved the respect for his own career. Had Rory said, "Postpone the Japanese tour," I think it would've worked. How long it would have lasted, I don't know, but I imagine it would've. With Keith, they had the same love for Muddy Waters and country & western music, there were a lot of similarities. Whether Rory's personality would've worked with the Stones is another story.

Rolling into Rotterdam

That three-day audition remains one of the big "what-ifs" in rock history. At the end of 1974, the Rolling Stones had lost Mick Taylor, who himself had replaced Brian Jones in 1969. Taylor was feeling stifled and wanted to spread his creative wings. The band had just released *It's Only Rock 'n' Roll* and were starting to work on what would become *Black and Blue* and had to find the perfect replacement. The list of potential candidates (some of them auditioned, others did not) reads like a who's who of '70s rock guitar: Jeff Beck, Peter Frampton, Nils Lofgren, Shuggie Ottis, Wayne Perkins, and Harvey Mandel (the last two actually appear on some tracks on *Black and Blue*). Rory certainly was part of the shortlist and had been on the Stones' radar for a while. In fact, they initially wanted to sign him as an artist on their label, Rolling Stones Records.

When Rory flew to Rotterdam, he brought a smaller amp: a Fender Deluxe tweed. That

amp has sometimes been presented as a 1954 model, but amps of that year still had the "wide panel" look. The "narrow panel" look of Rory's amp makes it a 1955 at the earliest. Back then, this 15-watt model was considered a student amp, not powerful enough for a larger stage, but a few players were starting to understand the value of a lower-powered amp to get crunch at a reasonable volume. Rory being Rory, he probably didn't want to drown the stage of the De Doelen concert hall with the volume of his two-amp rig of that era. The Deluxe was a reasonable choice, but it wasn't a sonic compromise either. In fact, Rory had used it for a few overdubs on his albums.

Ron Wood ended up joining the Rolling Stones, of course, and was officially presented as a member of the band in 1976 after having been part of the *Black and Blue* sessions and subsequent tour. Wood was far from a bad guitarist. In fact he proved to be a great riff player throughout the Faces' discography, but he was far from the stellar levels that Rory could reach. Wood was most likely hired to be a great team player and the perfect sparring partner for Keith Richards, all the more so since the two were already friends by then. Wood had little to no ego and wouldn't feel like the band was getting in the way of his solo career. He's still part of the Rolling Stones fifty years later.

The tapes of Rory's audition must be somewhere since the Rolling Stones had a habit of using their mobile studio to record everything they played. To this day, however, they have yet to surface.

JENSEN
SPECIAL DESIGN
SALES - SERVICE
PROFESSIONAL

TONE
INST. VOL.
MIC. VOL.

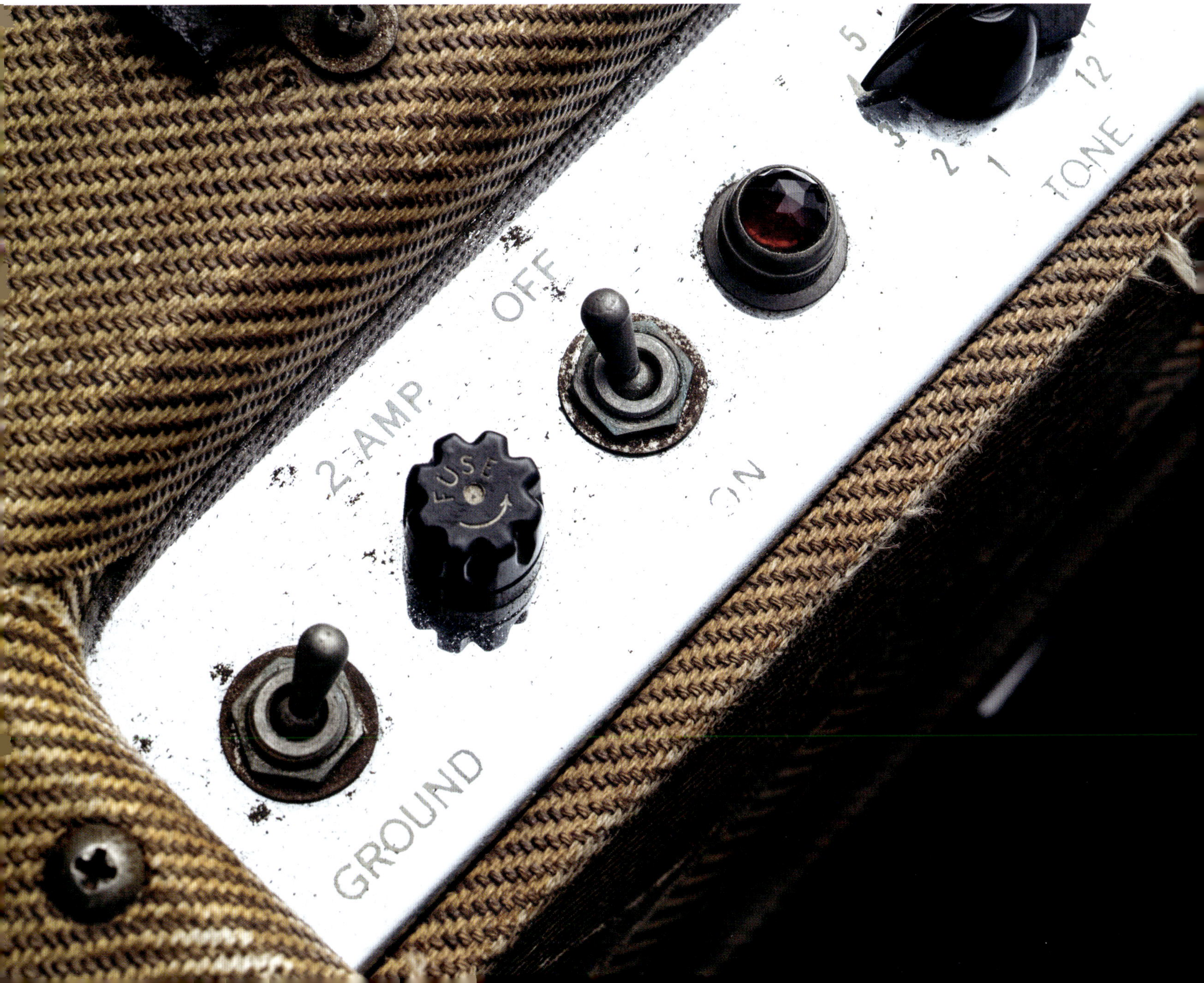

Keeping It Fun

Oahu Diana Deluxe Lap Steel
1961 Kay K1962 Value Leader
1967 Vox Mark XII Special
1976 Travis Bean TB500

Rory was a guitar collector through and through. He spent his life playing the same Stratocaster, but on the side he had more than a hundred instruments, all of which played a role in his artistry. While fronting Taste, he mostly used his main gear, but once he got his solo deal, he looked to diversify his sonic palette, especially in the studio.

With that tonal quest came the pure pleasure of collecting. At the time, few American-made guitars had crossed the ocean yet, and taking a trip to a US music store or pawnshop meant finding real artifacts from the land where the blues began. Little was known about "vintage" instruments at the time, and the very idea of writing a book about a bunch of cheap secondhand instruments would have seemed ludicrous.

Dónal Gallagher explains how Rory's collecting mind worked:

The collecting came from blues people that he respected, and from album covers where he'd see these guitars. He'd track one down to get the tone he heard on the record. He was always searching.

He was always after a bargain. He would leave gems behind because he felt the guy was asking too much. I'd see him leave the store and go off on the guy, go around the block and have a coffee, and the next thing you know he would get a call or he'd go back to the guy. He had to feel right about it or he wouldn't do it.

Judging from the collection featured in this book, he felt right about it pretty often.

Oahu Diana Deluxe Lap Steel

Rory wasn't known as a lap steel player. But judging from how musical he was playing slide on his Tele, he probably could hold his own with a steel bar, especially with a lap steel in a tuning that he was already familiar with, like open G. While his lap-steel playing hasn't been documented on record, at least two lap steels were part of his collection: a National Dynamic and this beautiful Oahu Diana Deluxe.

In the 1970s, vintage lap steels were extremely cheap and to this day remain the least expensive point of entry into vintage gear. They were extremely popular in the 1930s as part of the Hawaiian music craze and even played a significant part in the invention of the electric solidbody guitar, but by the 1970s no one knew what to do with them. Like the badge on the headstock says, Oahu (one of the main islands in Hawaii) was a music publishing company founded in the 1920s. They published instructional books that they sold along with their own instruments, which were manufactured by other companies. Lap steels like the Diana Deluxe, for example, were made in Chicago by the brand Kay.

As the name implies, the Diana Deluxe, also known as Tonemaster, was Oahu's top of the line, featuring a sunburst-finished mahogany body adorned with gold-leaf decals. The famous "string-through" Supro pickup is hidden under the wooden armrest, painted to match the rest of the body, and the Volume and Tone controls are placed on either side of it. The back reveals a nonslip pad that proved convenient when the Oahu rested on the player's lap.

The only known photo of Rory with this lap steel dates back to 1976, taken at Musicland Studios in Munich while he was working on the album that would become *Calling Card*. Instead of producing it himself, Rory enlisted the help of Roger Glover, the Deep Purple bass player who had been working on albums by Nazareth and Elf. The process was not an easy one. Glover tried to make the band sound more polished while Rory wanted to keep it raw. Perhaps the resulting tensions prompted Rory to pick up his lap steel to blow off steam between takes. Nevertheless, the resulting album is one of the most diverse and polished efforts in his discography.

OAHU PUBLISHING CO.
REG.U.S.
Oahu
CLEVELAND, O.
PAT.OFF

KAY

1961 Kay K1962 Value Leader

The way the Kay brand named its instruments could be confusing. Like Marshall, who had released the 1959 amp in 1967 and the 1962 amp in 1964, the K1962 was built in 1961.

Along with Harmony, Kay was one of the two biggest brands for US-made economy instruments. Founded in Chicago in 1931, they first built acoustic instruments and later got into the electric market, producing for other brands as well as under their own name. For instance, Kay also made Rory's Oahu lap steel.

The "Value Leader" name was used for a series of cheap electrics introduced by Kay in 1960. The model number indicated the number of "pancake" pickups in the guitar: a single neck pickup for the K1961, two pickups for the K1962, and three for the K1963. They look like regular solidbody instruments, but they're hollowbody thinline guitars without the classic telltale f-holes, which explains their light weight.

Rory bought this guitar in 1971 in New York City with a little help from John Hammond Jr., the famous blues singer and son of producer John H. Hammond. Hammond Jr. was one of the few musicians at the time who connected with Rory over a common passion for older instruments, and just like Rory, he played resonator guitars. Legend has it that Eric Clapton gave Hammond's number to Rory, who called up Hammond during a visit to meet record labels ahead of his debut solo album's release in April 1971. The two went guitar shopping on 11th Street in Greenwich Village. This might have been Unredeemed Pledge, a pawnbroker located on 11th and 3rd, a dangerous and downtrodden neighborhood at the time. Upstairs, Rory found this Kay K1962 and, according to Dónal Gallagher, Rory haggled the price down from to $50 after Hammond had unsuccessfully tried to reduce the price.

It *would* be fair to assume that Rory, being the blues scholar that he was, recognized a guitar made famous by the New Orleans bluesman Lonnie Johnson, whose solos are crucial to how the guitar went from a rhythmic to a melodic instrument. Rory probably knew that he was walking in Johnson's footsteps. It only made sense to make that symbolic connection more tangible by owning the same guitar.

1967 Vox Mark XII Special

As a Rolling Stones fan, Rory was taken by Brian Jones' sound, charisma, and blues skills. Jones was the true leader of the early Stones, the most experienced musician of the bunch, and a blues connoisseur. As such, he was instrumental in bringing slide playing to the British masses. And no other guitar is more synonymous with Brian Jones than the iconic Vox Mark VI, the famous white teardrop-shaped prototype that he used to play "Reelin' and Rockin'" as well as "Time Is on My Side" for the Stones' October 1964 performance on *The Ed Sullivan Show*.

Vox started building guitars in 1961. In 1962 they released the Phantom VI, a strange offset design that evolved into the Phantom Mark VI in 1963, then shortened into Mark VI. The success of the "teardrop" guitar was such that Vox couldn't build them fast enough out of their British facility, so they contracted them to Italian factories Eko and Crucianelli. In 1965, right after the smashing success of the Beatles' "Hard Day's Night" and its jangly twelve-string solo, Vox developed the Mark XII, a twelve-string version of the Mark VI, complete with a rare and weird twelve-string version of the Bigsby vibrato.

As an amp and pedal brand, Vox was keen on integrating electronics into their instruments, which they did with the "Special" versions of the Mark VI and Mark XII. These guitars were powered by a battery (whose trap access was hidden by a protective pad on the back side), and they had six built-in effects controlled by six switches, including several boosts, a fuzz, and a short echo (dubbed Repeat).

Rory bought his Vox Mark XII Special in 1978, but it is not known whether the vibrato arm had already been broken off or if he made the modification himself. The Vox saw a little live action, but it was used mostly in the studio, where Rory enjoyed the added harmonic content that a twelve-string instrument could bring to a track. Plus, it looks extremely cool.

VOX

FUZZ
SUSTAIN

MID
BOOST
SELECTOR
REPEAT
SPEED
FUZZ
SUSTAIN
P/U SELECTOR

VOX

TREBLE
BASS
TOP BOOST
MID BOOST
FUZZ
REPEAT
VOX

1976 Travis Bean TB500

While Rory was making waves in the mid to late 1970s, the guitar landscape was rapidly changing. The big brand names had all been bought out by large corporations that could not have cared less about the quality of the instruments they were shilling, which in turn made their older guitars more desirable and more expensive. At the same time, a few independent luthiers began to garner attention from the most demanding musicians who wanted nothing but the best—and wanted to be part of their instruments' creation. On the acoustic side of things, people like Bob Taylor, Michael Gurian, Bill Collings, Richard Hoover, James Goodall, and Stuart Mossman were inspired by prewar Martins but they also had their own ideas of what would make a great guitar. On the electric side, Alembic was the starting point of the boutique phenomenon. They came from Santa Rosa, California, and started out working for the Grateful Dead in 1969, building sound systems and modifying their instruments. The idea was to use the best woods available for the best possible tone and to integrate onboard EQs and effects to maximize versatility.

Travis Bean was another California luthier looking for a way to maximize resonance and sustain while making guitars less prone to neck action changes. He found it in 1974 with the help of his associate, Gary Kramer, by using a machined aluminum neck with an open headstock (featuring a T-shaped hole). Gary left to create his own brand, Kramer, which also started out by making aluminum-neck guitars. Meanwhile, Travis Bean Guitars has remained a low-profile operation that didn't get the resounding success it should have, despite being used by the likes of Keith Richards, Slash, and Steve Albini.

Rory Gallagher got this TB500, the "budget" version of this model (and also one of the rarest) as a gift from Bean himself, along with a handwritten letter, in 1976. This is one of the very first produced, bearing the serial number 17 (numbers started at 11). Jerry Garcia got number 12, and judging from the date embossed on top of the headstock, Rory's was built on 11-18-76. A regular production model would've had a "droopier" black pickguard, which makes this one all the more special. Rory did not use it much, probably because of its considerable weight.

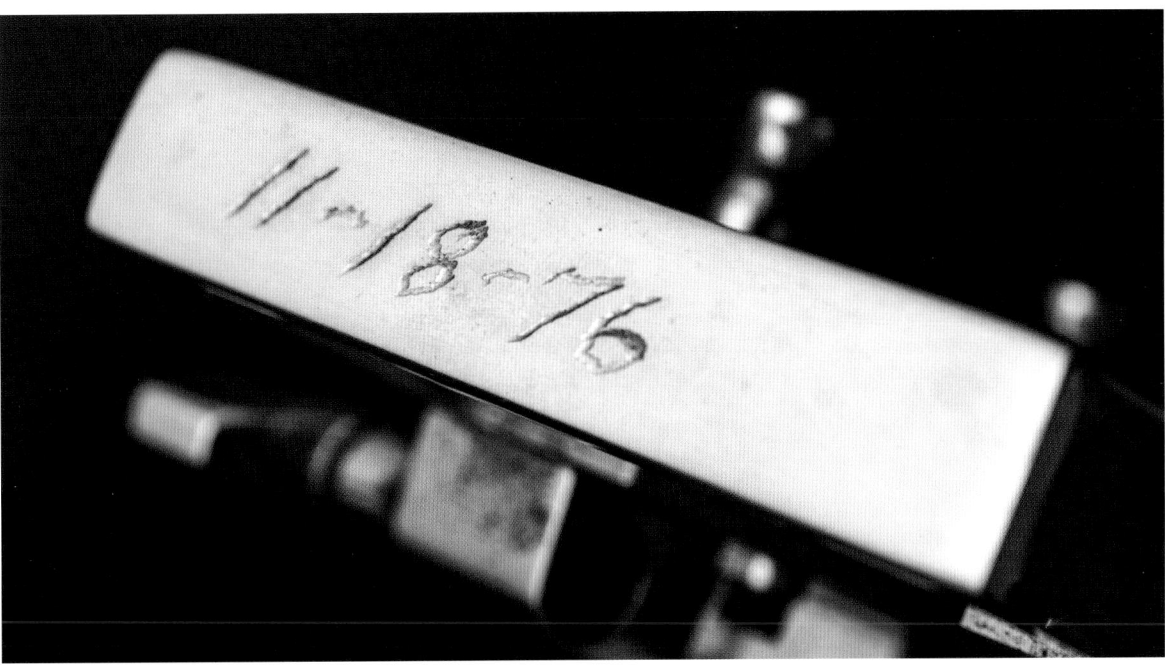

Notes from San Francisco

1976 Fender Telecaster Deluxe and 1958 Gibson Les Paul Junior

Fender
TELECASTER DELUXE

Fender®

After the disappointing experience of working with another producer on *Calling Card*, Rory probably wasn't too keen on doing it again. But his label really wanted an album they could promote in the US, something to "break" him in as an artist there. Rory chose to work with famed producer Elliot Mazer, who was mostly known for his work on several Neil Young albums. They got to work at the His Master's Wheels studio in San Francisco in December 1977 with the help of Rory's band. Things got complicated from the start because the gear was not functioning perfectly from having been moved around to record the Band's *The Last Waltz*. Rory also had a hard time letting go of the producer's job. The result was an album that sounds tame and slightly overproduced. What came out as *Notes from San Francisco* sounds a little like *Exile on Main St.* by the Rolling Stones—a classic rock album filled to the brim with honky-tonk piano that was a little out of touch with the many changes in the musical landscape of the late 1970s.

Dissatisfied, Rory scrapped the album, making it one of the great "lost albums" in rock history until it came out posthumously in 2011. He also decided to fire his band and go back to the original trio formula. Gerry McAvoy stayed as the bass player, but Rod de'Ath was replaced with Ted McKenna, a Scottish musician who previously played with the Sensational Alex Harvey Band.

1976 Fender Telecaster Deluxe

While he was recording what would become *Notes from San Francisco*, Rory was looking for instruments that would inspire him to try new sonic colors, he took a liking to the Fender Telecaster Deluxe.

The Deluxe is the last evolution of the classic Fender design that took place from the late 1960s to the early 1970s. Apart from a few details, the Telecaster had remained basically unchanged from its inception in 1950. Then, in 1968, Fender released the Thinline, a semi-hollow version with f-holes. In 1971, the Thinline Tele became the first model to receive Fender's brand-new pickup, the Wide Range humbucker. Wanting to get into the humbucker game to keep up with Gibson, Fender hired Seth Lover, the very engineer who had come up with the original Gibson humbucker (nicknamed the "PAF" for Patent Applied For). Fender and Lover didn't want a copy of the Gibson pickup, so they devised a magnet made of an alloy named CuNiFe (Copper, Nickel, and Iron) for a humbucker with an open and airy sound.

The Wide Range pickup first appeared on the Thinline, but it became a defining element of the Telecaster Custom launched in 1972, a

new model with a larger pickguard, a humbucker in the neck position, a toggle switch on the upper bout, and four controls (probably a way of wooing Gibson fans). The Telecaster Deluxe followed suit in 1973 with the same specs except for *two* Wide Range pickups and a large Strat-style headstock.

Rory's Telecaster Deluxe is typical of the era, especially with the Mocha Brown finish that was launched in 1973 and screams "'70s cool." The controls have been modified to get closer to the classic Tele setup: the toggle switch has been moved near the other controls, of which there are only two: a Volume and a Tone. The original "witch hat" knobs have been replaced with classic "flat-top" Tele knobs, which was already the case on pictures dating back to 1978. Also, the neck pocket is much too wide for the neck, which was typical of Fender's quality control of the era.

It didn't seem to deter Rory from making some great music with it. Prior to that, he almost exclusively used single-coil guitars, but this Telecaster Deluxe brought the humbucker into his vocabulary.

1958 Gibson Les Paul Junior

During the recording of the lost album that would eventually become *Notes from San Francisco*, Rory did some guitar shopping, picking up the previously seen Telecaster Deluxe as well as this 1958 Les Paul Junior.

The Les Paul Junior came out in 1954 as a way of making the Les Paul design more accessible to beginners and budding musicians. The Standard model had been out for two years when Gibson introduced both the top-of-the-line Custom and the $99 entry-level Junior. The Junior was spartan in its appearance and build, with a slab mahogany body without a maple top, a silkscreen logo, a Sunburst finish (instead of the Goldtop finish of the Standard), dot neck markers, and no binding. And even though Gibson introduced upgrades on the more expensive models, the Junior kept the single-coil P-90 when the humbucker arrived in 1957, and the wraparound bridge didn't get the Tune-O-Matic upgrade in 1955.

As such, the Junior was long overlooked as a lesser version of the Les Paul, even though it was made with the same craftsmanship and materials as the upper-end models. It took the outside-the-box thinking of guitar hero Leslie West from Mountain to show the world just how good a Junior could sound in the right hands. Other players like Keith Richards and Johnny Thunders took notice.

Rory was also touched by the masterful efficiency of the Junior. In fact, it was the only Les Paul he ever owned, probably deterred by the cliché baggage of the Standard 'Burst and the fanciness of the Custom. Apart from the similarly econo Melody Maker, the Junior was the only Gibson model Rory played.

This Junior bears the serial number 84374, which indicates it was made in 1958, meaning it was one of the last single-cut Juniors before Gibson switched to the double-cutaway shape that same year. Being an instrument actually used by Rory, this Junior has been modded and repaired: the knobs are not original, the tuners have been changed (probably several times given the holes left on the headstock) before settling on Schallers, and most importantly and significantly, the bridge has been changed for a Leo Quan Badass. The Leo Quan brand was launched in 1972 by Leo Malliaris and Glen Quan, who designed a better bridge for the Fender bass and a better version of the Gibson wraparound that could compensate for any intonation issues. That is the bridge seen here, in a gold-plated version that looks quite out of place on the austere Junior. Either the bridge was already there when Rory bought the guitar or it was all he could find when he decided to replace the previous bridge.

Either way, this Junior did not see too much action in 1977–1978, but Rory got around to using it in 1990 during the recording of his last album, *Fresh Evidence*. It can be heard on two songs, "Kid Gloves" and "Walkin' Wounded," on which he gets that gritty crunchy sound typical of early Faces albums.

Custom Made

1974 Guyatone Rory Gallagher Model
1972 Eccleshall Mandola
1970s Eccleshall Electric Guitar
1980s Eccleshall T-Style Electric Guitar

REV

NOR
REV

With a certain level of fame and recognition comes the opportunity to commission custom-made instruments that perfectly complement one's playing style and sonic desires. Some artists have turned to luthiers, like Jerry Garcia with his Doug Irwin Tiger guitar or Ron Wood and his Zemaitis, while others have designed signature models in collaboration with brands, like Les Paul with Gibson or Chet Atkins with Gretsch. Rory Gallagher dabbled in both sides of the equation, but he was ultimately so comfortable with his faithful Stratocaster that he didn't really have much use for any other instrument.

1974 Guyatone Rory Gallagher Model

This is the only Rory Gallagher model that he developed with any brand (his Fender replica was a posthumous model). This Guyatone came about in the era of the Japanese takeover on the electric guitar market, with brands looking for famous rock musicians to help sell their guitars, but also give them the credibility they needed to convince the world that they were producing quality instruments. Ibanez had the Bob Weir model in 1975, followed by the George Benson model in 1977 (they also tried, but failed, to get Jeff Beck as a signature artist in 1979). Guyatone wanted Rory, which made sense since Rory had already played an LG-60B model.

Guyatone got to work in 1974 and finally gave the Rory Gallagher Model to its namesake upon his arrival at the Tokyo airport in January 1975. The guitar is a complete anomaly within the Gallagher collection, and it bears hardly any resemblance to any other guitar that Rory would usually play. The asymmetrical body with a wide pickguard is closer to an Epiphone Coronet than a Strat, the semi-through-neck has a binding and an ebony fretboard, and it has a single humbucker pickup, all of which make for a unique guitar. Either Rory—who favored single-coil pickups and bolt-on necks with rosewood fretboards—didn't get his say in designing the guitar or he wanted to try something completely different. The reverse headstock is particularly surprising: it has become a metal guitar cliché in the years since, but in 1975 no other brand was doing it. The only prior inspiration (aside, perhaps, from Jimi Hendrix playing a right-handed Strat upside down) was the first version of the Gibson Firebird (made from 1963 to 1965), which may also have been where Guyatone got the idea of a through-neck. The bridge is the Leo Quan Badass version of the wraparound, and the truss rod cover on the headstock bears Rory's name. Finally, the guitar also has a switch next to the Volume and Tone controls to go from "NOR" to "REV"—"NOR" is probably "Normal," but "REV" is anybody's guess, especially on a single-pickup guitar that doesn't leave much room for switching options.

On the night he was given this Guyatone signature model, Rory used it during his show in Shibuya, but only for the slide songs. No guitar, however local it may have been, could dethrone the Strat.

Rory Gallagher

1972 Eccleshall Mandola

It would be an understatement to call Rory Gallagher a hard-working musician. He released eleven albums in nineteen years and played anywhere from 60 to 125 shows a year. That kind of workload takes its toll on instruments, especially when one instrument in particular is used ninety percent of the time. Rory needed a proper guitar tech and caretaker for his Strat and the rest of his collection, and he found the partner he needed in Chris Eccleshall.

Eccleshall learned his craft by working as a violin maker, and when he moved on to the guitar his first significant customer was Rory himself. "Rory Gallagher was the first main customer," Eccleshall recalled. "He phoned me up at home one day and said he had a lot of stuff that needed sorting out, so that was about two month's work in itself." The phone call happened in 1971, right when Gallagher was about to launch his solo career and needed his gear in proper working order.

Eccleshall also worked for customers such as Pete Townshend (for whom he would repair guitars smashed on stage), David Bowie, the Sweet, Paul Weller, and others, but his relationship with Rory was the longest and most intense. Eccleshall was Rory's favored tech from 1971 to 1985, and during that period he kept the Strat in proper working order, for instance by drying up the neck to keep the moisture away and refretting it a grand total of eighteen times. He was also responsible for ensuring the vibrato was blocked by putting a piece of wood behind it. Rory never used the vibrato, and having it floating around added to the tension of the strings and put the guitar out of tune when a string broke. Blocking the vibrato provided constant tension and a better transmission of the sound to the body.

We can also infer that Eccleshall was responsible for most of the mods on the guitars

CE
C J ECCLESHALL
LONDON ENGLAND

in Rory's collection, even though he was a discrete helper and didn't brag about his achievements by the musician's side.

Eccleshall did leave a few concrete marks while at Rory's side, however, in the form of five custom-built instruments, three of which are featured here.

The Eccleshall mandola is most likely the first instrument built by Eccleshall for Rory. It is a larger cousin of the mandolin, usually tuned a fifth lower even though it seems that Rory tuned this one even lower. It is a gorgeous instrument whose stunning figured Brazilian rosewood back gives away Eccleshall's experience as a violin marker. Its serial number, 0048, is also a proof of how green the luthier was when Rory first met him.

The mandola is amplified with the same Ibanez pickup as Rory's Martin mandolin, but Eccleshall also built Rory a proper solidbody electric mandola during the same period. The electric mandola has a single neck pickup that has been changed over time, until landing on the Tele-style pickup it has today.

RHYTHM

1970s Eccleshall Electric Guitar

This is the main Eccleshall electric guitar custom-made for Rory Gallagher. Its bizarre shape was probably inspired by a guitar that Rory was quite fond of—the Japanese-made Guyatone LG-60B—while a slightly more elegant headstock shape evokes the non-reverse version of the Gibson Firebird (built from 1965 to 1969) and the Gibson Trini Lopez Standard. Even the pickguard shape is the same as the LG-60B, down to the smaller white pickguard on top of the large black pickguard. The bridge seems to have been changed several times before settling on the Tune-O-Matic, the telltale signs being the black plastic parts covering holes on both sides of the bridge, and also the string ferrules at the back of the body, rendered useless by the current bridge. There is a fret zero in typical '70s luthier fashion, as well as two blade pickups. Finally, the serial number is A198, which should be proof that it was built after the mandola.

1980s Eccleshall T-Style Electric Guitar

This is the last guitar that Eccleshall built for Rory, and it was commissioned by a fan as a gift (the neckplate reads, "C313 / Presented to Rory Gallagher by Gordon Morris / Eccleshall Guitars"). And it's a really nice gift too: a tobacco sunburst Tele-style body with an ebony fretboard and two humbuckers. Rory called them "Gibson PAFs" in an interview, so they could have been salvaged from a late-50s/early-60s Gibson, but he could also have been using the term as a generic way of alluding to a humbucker pickup. In fact, their cream color makes them look like DiMarzios, pickups that luthier would commonly have had access to at the time. As a nice bonus, the extra-slim neck is made of a beautiful piece of bird's-eye maple.

This Tele-style guitar can be heard on the song "Continental Op" from the album *Defender* (1987), where it sounds nice and fat with that typical Tele spank.

1978-1990

From Photo Finish to Fresh Evidence

Getting Harder

1978 / 1980 Marshall 2104 Combos and Pedalboards

Marshall

ENCE
BASS

After the late-1977 debacle of recording what would become *Notes from San Francisco*, Rory decided not to work with another outside producer again and went back to his original trio formula. Gerry McAvoy was still on bass duty, but the new drummer was Ted McKenna, an absolute hard hitter even by Gallagher's standards. The newly formed trio flew to a studio in Cologne, Germany, in the summer of 1978, this time with Rory producing. The resulting album, *Photo-Finish*, is a true testament to Rory's ability to stay in touch with the times. He was a student of the blues, but he wasn't a purist, and *Photo-Finish* is the sound of a musician doing his best to stay relevant at a time when the music landscape was moving at a dizzying pace. While recording in San Francisco, Rory had seen the Sex Pistols' "last concert" on January 14, 1978, at the Winterland Ballroom. The experience was a shock to him, and the raw energy of the British punks was a big part of what made him question the result of the recording sessions he was doing at the time. It seemed like everyone else was moving fast: fellow Irishmen Thin Lizzy had just released *Bad Reputation*, their heaviest album yet. After producing Rory's *Calling Card*, Roger Glover had gone on to produce an up-and-coming Birmingham band's third album, *Sin After Sin* by Judas Priest, which together with Motörhead's 1977 self-titled debut album marked the early signs of the New Wave of British Heavy Metal. Tempos were getting faster, riffs were getting harder, and walls of Marshall stacks were delivering bigger and brighter sounds.

From the get-go, *Photo-Finish* takes no prisoners, and the opening track, the aptly named "Shin-Kicker," leads the charge with a straight-ahead rock 'n' roll riff. McKenna bashes away as he joins, slightly on top of the beat—no piano, no breakdown. In fact, *Photo-Finish* is Rory's first album without a single acoustic song. And of course, as the sound of his music evolved, the gear had to follow suit.

1978 / 1980 Marshall 2104 Combos

The first evolution sound came with the purchase of a new amp, a Fender brownface Concert. Brownface Fenders are the transitional stage between the crunchy tweed era and the cleaner blackface era, and the Concert is a beast with 40 watts of power through four 10-inch speakers. He boosted it with the Hawk II and blended it with the Bassman. Later in 1978, he started playing an Ampeg VT-40 on stage. The American brand is mostly known for classic bass models like the B-15

JMP
SERIAL No:-
03424L
0
1
POWER
0
1
STANDBY
PRESENCE
0
2
4
6
10

BASS INPUT LEAD
EQUALIZER
ATTACK+EQ.
DIST.+EQ.
MIN.
MAX.
100
+12dB
0dB
-12dB
BOSS Driver DB-5
SOUND INNOVATOR
BOSS
NORMAL
3722

and the behemoth SVT (Gerry McAvoy's amp of choice), but their guitar amps have always been a secret weapon for players like Keith Richards and Johnny Winter. Rory found they would go into overdrive more easily than his usual Fenders—especially when boosted with the Hawk II—with a nice mid-forward character that helped him rise above McKenna's energetic drumming.

Rory achieved the last step of his transition to a heavier hard rock sound on the 1980 live album *Stage Struck*. It opens, like *Photo-Finish*, with "Shin-Kicker," except this version is faster, feels even more urgent and alive, and his sound is more distorted, fatter, and more cutting at the same time. Rory always used pinch harmonics, but with that new sound they seemed to scream and fly out of the record's groove. That newfound enthusiasm is unmistakable on a song like "Bad Penny" (from the 1999 reissue), where Rory revels in the simplicity of the trio formula. The rest of the decade would be more complicated and filled with self-doubt, though: from 1971 to 1979 he released ten solo albums but would only turn out three during the 1980s.

Stage Struck is the first album featuring Rory's brand-new rig in the form of two Marshall 50-watt combos. Jim Marshall was a drummer and music-shop owner who started out copying Fender amps in the early 1960s because they were too expensive to import and then went on to design his own circuits. The demand from users such as Pete Townshend, Eric Clapton, and Jimi Hendrix pushed him to create bigger and louder amps, so much so that in the 1970s, a wall of Marshall stacks was the way to go for any hard rock band worth its salt. With roots firmly planted in the blues, Rory had always stayed away from that cliché, but he finally went the Marshall route in 1980. He didn't use the same stack as everyone else though: most Marshall players were using the Super Lead (the original 100-watt monster of the late 1960s) or the JMP head, but Rory loved combos and had been using them since the beginning of his career, so he picked two 2104 combos, 50-watt combo versions of the JMP head. The JMP, launched in 1976, was the first generation of Marshall amps with a Master Volume (i.e., with separate Gain and Volume controls to reach a more overdriven sound without necessarily going for a deafening volume). Choosing the 50-watt combo (instead of the more common 100-watt version) was also a way of getting the power tubes to distort more quickly, and the two 12-inch speakers must've seemed quite familiar to Rory, since his AC30s had the same configuration.

Because the Marshalls could produce a massive amount of overdrive on their own, Rory no longer needed the help of his Rangemaster or Hawk II booster. He just needed to correct the frequency response ever-so-slightly with the help of a BOSS graphic equalizer, first a big bulky DB-5, then the compact EQ-6 pedal, to push the mediums and tame the highs, keeping the sound from getting shrill.

As to why he used *two* Marshalls simultaneously on stage, it must be because he had gotten used to the stereo image he got from his previous two-amp setups. Even though he had doubled the same amp model, having two still meant a wider sound diffusion and enough volume to compete with a bashing drummer.

In 1987, Rory went back to an AC30 coupled with one of the Marshall combos. He would also add a proper Marshall stack to add some bottom end, a JMP Super Bass (the bass version of the JMP head) with a 4x12 cabinet. Once he went the Marshall route, there seemed to be no going back.

Pedalboards

Rory was not a big effects guy. Unlike many other players, he would not rely on any pedal or rack unit to get his sound. In fact, he almost seemed proud of his "it's all in the hands" approach. He never used fuzz (even though the Rangemaster could get pretty fuzzy at times), never used a wah (unlike so many of his peers), and never got into the ultra-clean and ultra-saturated overcompressed sounds of the 1980s. He was a big proponent of getting overdrive from the amp without

the help of a pedal and of getting a wah effect from the Tone control on his Strat.

But looking through the crates of gear while the Bonhams staff prepared the displays for the 2024 auction, it quickly became apparent that there was more to it than Rory would admit. The man owned more than a few effects—a hundred pedals, maybe more. Everything from a full collection of plug-in Dan Armstrong boxes to tape echoes, racks, weird Electro-Harmonix models from the 1970s, a rare Tycobrahe Octavia . . . it seems that Rory was with effects as he was with guitars: he used few of them in public, but it certainly didn't keep him from collecting them.

During the 1980s, he started using a few pedals more regularly to complement the sound of his two Marshall combos. First, he toyed with the classic MXR Phase 90, but other players had used it so much that he consciously avoided that extremely recognizable sound. Then, he moved on to the BOSS Flanger, the classic BF-2. The flanger was a relatively new effect at the time, and it wasn't as cliché as the phaser had become, especially when used as sparingly as Rory did. It can be clearly heard on "Moonchild" off *Stage Struck* (a song that clearly inspired Iron Maiden's "Two Minutes to Midnight," but that's another story). It could very well be the BOSS BF-1 heard here, the bigger previous version that was introduced in 1976, since the BF-2 came out only months before the live album was released.

At that point, the BF-2 became part of Rory's arsenal for good and he got himself a "proper" pedalboard in the mid-1980s. At the same time, most players were using massive racks, and pedals were mostly seen as a thing of the past. There was no such thing as buying a pedalboard, so Rory built it from wooden boards covered with black tape. He didn't use a daisy-chain power supply that would have made his life much easier: all the pedals were powered by batteries to avoid any ground loop noise. The four pedals featured on his board were an MXR Dyna Comp, an Ibanez TS-808 Tube Screamer, the aforementioned BOSS BF-2 Flanger, and a BOSS OC-2 Octaver (which came out in 1984). The Dyna Comp, one of the first MXR pedals released in 1974, was a compressor but Rory didn't use it as an audible compression effect. He left it on all the time to compensate for the lengthy cables he used on stage. Basically, this was his buffer. He would kick in the Tube Screamer to boost the gain for his solos, and when that one broke down he replaced it with a BOSS OD-1 Overdrive, a close cousin of the Ibanez. Finally, the Octaver was the special bonus effect that he would kick in every once in a while. It can clearly be heard on the 1990 song "The Loop" off *Fresh Evidence*, and on the 1985 version of "Philby" live at the Montreux Festival, combined with either a flanger or an envelope filter (maybe a BOSS TW-1).

Rory treated his effects like the rest of his rig: a few immovable mainstays and whatever else would tickle his fancy at the time, without any hard rules.

Marshall

The Other Strat

1958 Fender Stratocaster

TONE

Rory Gallagher is one of the main artists who put the Stratocaster on the map and turned it into the legendary instrument it is today. But his collection didn't include multiple versions of the Strat. In fact, he only used three: his main '61, the 1979 Anniversary (more on that in the epilogue addressing "Rory's Legacy"), and the 1958 seen here. By comparison, Hendrix used more than a dozen Strats during his four-year solo career, David Gilmour sold at least twenty-five Strats at auction in 2019, and the 2025 Jeff Beck auction saw twenty Strats go to new owners.

Rory's passion for the Strat was mostly a one-guitar affair, but he couldn't pass on the opportunity of owning another fine example. Actually, he could if the deal didn't feel right. As previously explained, Rory loved to haggle and wanted to get the right deals on the guitars he bought. As Dónal Gallagher recalls, that's why he didn't acquire the twin to his '61: "There was a sunburst Stratocaster just a few digits off his own, somewhere in Texas. The idea was to get it as a backup guitar. He just felt the guy was putting too much of a premium on it."

It makes a lot of sense that the seller would ask for an exorbitant price, since it was the '61's identical twin and hence the perfect backup should anything happen to it.

A Vastly Different Strat

The right opportunity presented itself in 1976 while Rory was touring the US. He encountered a guitar salesman named—as fate would have it—Robert Johnson, who had a 1958 Stratocaster for sale. It's impossible to know whether it was presented as a '57 or '58 at the time, since Rory would use both dates depending on the interview. In retrospect, it definitely looks like a 1958 since the Sunburst has red in it, starting to veer toward the three-tone hue of '60s Strat rather than the traditional two-tone look of the 1950s. The three-ply pickguard is also a telltale sign of a late-'50s Strat (a '57 would have a one-ply guard) even though it could have changed since it seems to have a one-ply on some pictures. Also, the neck profile is on the slimmer side while a '57 neck is usually a nice chunky V. The 30453 serial number is another clue, but the ultimate confirmation is the date on the heel of the neck that says 10-58 for October 1958. The fact that this is a late '58 explains the specs usually associated with a '59, like the sunburst hue and the three-ply pickguard.

Rory could have been deterred by the fact that this was a vastly different Strat from his main one, especially with the maple fretboard instead of the rosewood he was used to. But his love of Buddy Holly made him close the deal. He did his usual modifications to make it work for him, starting by locking off the

Fender STRATOCASTER
WITH SYNCHRONIZED TREMOLO
ORIGINAL
Contour
Body

vibrato with a block of wood. By 1976 he was probably used to it, having done the same thing to his main Strat back in the 1960s, much to Dónal's surprise (see page 17).

He also had the guitar refretted with jumbo frets to suit his playing style and his love of bends, and the wiring was modified to bypass the Tone control for the middle pickup (the lower knob, which looks quite new compared with the other two).

Even though Rory didn't need a backup Strat, he ended up playing the '58 for its own sonic merit. Its stinging quality can be heard on the song "I Ain't No Saint" from the 1987 album *Defender*, and he started using its brighter and snappier sound on stage for the 1988 shows. Compared with the '61, it looks new, but it has the few signs of an instrument that has seen its fair share of stage action: the pickguard is worn right next to the truss rod access (which shows it has been set up many times), the pick scratches have dug a small trench into the wood above the pickguard, and there's a little bit of the blue denim hue on the back.

The 1958 may not have been one of his most played guitars, but being the backup Strat for an icon like Rory's '61 is still extremely high praise.

Modded Tools

1963 Gretsch 6135 Corvette
1960 Silvertone 1303
1978 Fender Musicmaster
1957 Rickenbacker Combo 400
1960 Gibson Melody Maker

BURNS

BURNS
U.S.PAT

The main criterion separating Rory Gallagher from most collectors is that he used most of the guitars he owned. Even when the vintage niche was becoming a big-dollar market, he was never precious about keeping the original parts for any guitar. In fact, while looking through his collection, I found a vibrato arm in the case of the white Telecaster, which shows how little he cared about the spare parts once he had gotten an instrument set up the way he wanted it. He wasn't about finding pristine premium examples of rare instruments, but rather about getting good deals on interesting guitars and making them work for his playing.

As such, most instruments in his collection are modified, either by Chris Eccleshall or Rory himself. Those mods can be as small as changing a broken tuner or as massive as changing a bridge, refinishing, or adding a pickup in a spot where there wasn't supposed to be one in the first place. It was not out of vanity either: Rory had a practical approach, and he evaluated what needed to be done to make the instrument suit his taste. He experimented and sometimes he tripped and fell, like when he tried to add a middle pickup to both the black Esquire and the white Tele. But the instruments he played the most have all been modded. They were the tools of his trade and needed to perform aptly for the job at hand. As previously seen, even modifying a precious vintage piece like the '58 Strat was fair game if it meant it would get played. Even a seemingly lowly cheap Gretsch deserved a few modifications if he found it inspiring enough.

1963 Gretsch 6135 Corvette

Dónal remembers finding the 1963 Gretsch Corvette in the window of a pawnshop in downtown Los Angeles while out shopping for guitars in the late 1970s. Rory did a three-date residency at the Starwood in Hollywood at the end of 1978, which was most likely when the deed was done. Dónal didn't know anything about the Corvette, so he haggled without having any real intention of buying. But when he got the price down from $75 to only $50, the deal was too good to pass. When Rory learned about it and saw the guitar, he was incredibly pleased. Even though the Corvette has never been a highly sought-after Gretsch, $50 is roughly the equivalent of $250 in today's money—too good to pass, indeed.

The Corvette was Gretsch's first proper solidbody. The Duo Jet, introduced in 1953, had been presented as the solidbody rival to Gibson's Les Paul, but it was more of a semi-hollowbody with no f-holes. The Corvette, introduced in 1961, is all solid, and it bears more than a passing resemblance to Gibson's SG introduced earlier that same year as the new Les Paul shape, from the two pointy cutaways to the red finish on the contoured mahogany body. Unlike the SG, though, the

Corvette was an entry-level instrument in the Gretsch catalog, an alternative to Gibson's Les Paul Junior with minimal ornaments, including dot neck markers. Several models were introduced in the Corvette line: the 6132 (red, one pickup, tailpiece bridge), the 6133 (platinum, one pickup, tailpiece), the 6134 presented here (red, one pickup, Burns vibrato), and the 6135 (red, two pickups, vibrato). There were also two additional color schemes that had their own names: the white 6106 Princess and the 6109 Peppermint Twist, red with a striped pickguard. The Corvette was never a classic or successful model, but it has remained a wonderful pawnshop find through the years.

Rory became a quick convert to the Corvette's understated charm and found it especially useful for slide playing. In fact, it ended up superseding the black Esquire as his main slide guitar in the late 1970s, which explains the extra heavy strings he used. In its road case there were a few spare Fender strings with gauges 013, 015, and 018, which were most likely

used, respectively, for the high E, the B, and the G strings. To become the tool Rory needed, the Corvette went through a lot: changed Schaller tuners ("made in West Germany," a sign of the times!), broken-off vibrato arm, bridge changed for a tune-o-matic harmonica style, and a new pickup.

The original pickup on the Corvette was the Gretsch HiLo'Tron, a single-coil that looks a lot like a mini humbucker but has an impressively low output level. This gives it a nice blooming bright character, but it has so little output that most players have changed it at some point. Rory was no exception, opting for a Gibson P-90 and turning the Corvette into a Les Paul Junior in all but name. The pickup was poorly installed with gaps all around it (since the original was a little larger), and it is slightly slanted, which means the strings are not facing the magnets. This really didn't seem to bother Rory, who gave the Corvette an enviable spot as one of his main touring instruments, in Guitar Trunk Number One.

1960 Silvertone 1303

Among the many beautiful, heavily modded pawnshop guitars in Rory's collection, this Silvertone takes the cake in more ways than one.

First, the model itself: Silvertone is arguably the ultimate department-store guitar brand. The name was created by the Sears, Roebuck and Co., but the instruments were manufactured in several factories during the 1950s and 1960s, including Harmony, Kay, and in this case, Danelectro. This makes for a vast array of models produced, which often leads to confusion, especially since the Silvertone brand hasn't been studied by vintage enthusiasts with the same attention to details as the big-name brands. Even though this Silvertone has been officially presented as a 1360 model, it is most likely a 1303 (or U2 in the Danelectro catalog). The 1360 was an exceedingly rare model with a smaller, more compact body. This one has all the classic attributes of a 1303, including the "dolphin-nose" headstock, minus the metal logo, which has been lost on many guitars.

Second, this is one of the most heavily modified guitars in Rory's collection. That funky purple metalflake finish certainly wasn't there when the Silvertone left the factory in 1960. It would have been either black or copper, and it seems to have some copper showing in some spots under the purple and gold layers. The refinish job is a pretty sloppy one, too: even the strap button on the upper bout has been painted, whereas most luthiers would have taken the time to remove any hardware before painting.

Nor are the pickups original. A Danelectro-made Silvertone had the famous lipstick pickups at that time, but this one has two

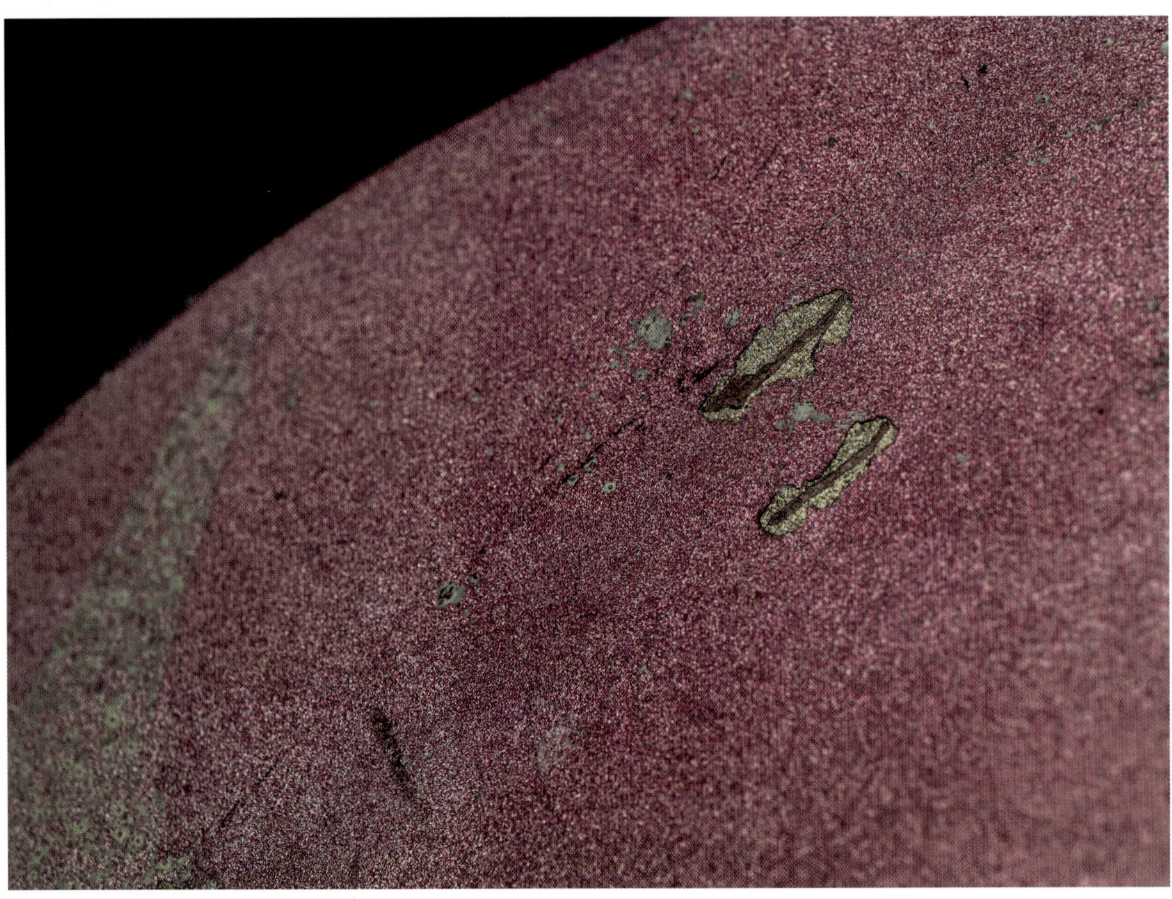

regular Fender-like single-coils with strange magnets that look like hex-key screws and individual surrounding cream pickguards. The knobs have also been changed for Gibson-like black speed knobs. Finally, the bridge is not original, either. It closely resembles Fender's hardtail bridge on the non-vibrato Stratocasters, and the strings are mounted through six ferrules added in the back of the body (with their own added black pickguard).

It is not known whether Rory used this guitar on any recordings after buying it in London in the 1980s. He also had an all-original 1961 Silvertone 1415 model that can be heard on "A Million Miles Away" and "Cradle Rock," which currently resides in the Johnny Marr collection, and also an all-original 1959 black example (with a broken logo) that was part of the 2024 auction. But this funky contraption is as Rory as it gets.

1978 Fender Musicmaster

This Musicmaster is another beautiful weirdo in the Rory Gallagher collection. It has actually seen some stage action, even being used as a spare for the '61 Strat for a few shows. It can be seen on the televised German show Rockpalast in 1982, while touring the *Jinx* album. Of course, Rory makes it sound remarkably close to his main guitar, only slightly darker.

Fender began producing the Musicmaster in 1956, hot on the heels of the Telecaster and the Stratocaster. Along with its two-pickup counterpart, the Duo-Sonic, the Musicmaster was Fender's first "student" model, a cheaper guitar with a short scale. In 1964, the pair received major upgrades that made them more like the Mustang, which had been introduced that same year.

This 1978 Musicmaster has the typical Mustang body and bigger headstock of that second version. It was originally white and has yellowed with age. The F tuners, bridge, and black pickguard are all original, but the pickups have been changed. The original black neck pickup has been replaced by a cream one with visible poles, while a bridge pickup has been added along with its own little black mounting pickguard. The luthier job was not so great and the angle of the two pickups is not the same, which probably wasn't intentional. There's also an additional round unfilled hole above the Volume knob. The hole was already present when the Musicmaster first appeared in pictures back in 1982, so we can only infer as to what was there before. Maybe the added three-way switch was placed there before being moved to the upper bout. It's yet another one of Rory's little secrets . . . .

Fender
MUSICMASTER

VOLUME

1957 Rickenbacker Combo 400

At first glance, Rory wouldn't seem like your typical Rickenbacker player. The California brand is usually associated with British Invasion artists (the Beatles), Mods (the Jam), and US jangle pop (the Byrds). The Combo models in particular are seldom seen in the hands of rock artists, with the noticeable exception of Cheap Trick's Robin Zander.

Rickenbacker Combos were launched in 1956 as a way for the brand to throw its hat in the ring of the blooming solidbody market. But they did it their way, with the help of German designer Roger Rossmeisl, who created a totally unique visual style for Rickenbacker. The Combo 400 has a double-cutaway "tulip" body with a through-neck that becomes the center part of the body (hence the clear zone below the bridge). The large pickguard is anodized gold on Rory's guitar, with the guitar itself in an unusual finish called Montezuma Brown.

Rory bought his Rickenbacker around 1978, probably more as a fun addition to the roster and because of the unusual aspect of the instrument rather than with the notion to actually use it on stage. He still managed to make it his own in a very visible way. The tuners have been changed into Schallers, the bridge is a Gibson-style tune-o-matic, and there's been an extra oh-so-slightly slanted bridge pickup added with its own extra pickguard. Finally, there are no fewer than five extra holes in the pickguard, including one that's been filled, with no clear explanation of what they were supposed to be. The regular controls are still in place, so it's really anybody's guess. One thing is for certain, though: it would have been interesting to hear Rory play this decidedly non-blues guitar.

Rickenbacker

Rickenbacker

1960 Gibson Melody Maker

The Gibson Melody Maker was a model that seemed to resonate with Rory. In fact, he ended up owning a few, including two later double-cutaway models (one modded with a bridge P-90) and this single-cut model.

The Melody Maker was Gibson's way of staying relevant for beginners and students in 1959. At the time, cheaper brands like Kay and Harmony were starting to make waves. Even the Les Paul Junior seemed expensive in comparison. So Gibson designed the Melody Maker with the $99 price point in mind, cutting even more corners on the Junior: the body is significantly thinner, the pickup is a small Fender-like single-coil instead of the Junior's P-90, and the wiring is mounted on the pickguard to facilitate final assembly. The shape of the Melody Maker went from one cutaway to two in 1962, before switching to two SG-like pointy cutaways in 1966 for the last version of the model.

This Melody Maker is the earlier single-cut version, modded with a humbucker instead of the original single-coil, and with Schaller tuners and a Leo Quan–style adjustable bridge. The humbucker modification turns it into a thinner, hot-rodded Les Paul Junior, and it has become a popular way of using the Melody Maker to get that vintage mahogany slab sound without the Junior price tag. Joan Jett, Pat Travers, and Norbert Krief are among the many musicians who have used mods to turn the Melody Maker into a legit pro instrument.

This Melody Maker entered Rory's world in 1985 (its headstock might not have been broken yet), and he would use it for slide but also in standard tuning for the bluesier songs in his live sets, when he needed a fatter and darker sound than his '61 Strat. For instance, in 1986, he played the Melody Maker on a scorching version of Muddy Waters' "I'm Ready" at a German festival. In March 1991 when Rory played at the Roxy Theatre in Los Angeles, Guns N' Roses guitarist Slash was there to meet one of his heroes. They ended up jamming together: Rory used his Gretsch Corvette and chose the Melody Maker for Slash, thinking he would enjoy the quirky but efficient little Gibson. And of course, he was right.

RANGEMASTER
VOX
VOX
MELODY MAKER
A.C. 30 TOP BOOST

Gibson

Replacing Old Faithful

Washburn Tanglewood
Takamine Dreadnought
Charvel 625C

While Rory's collecting habit was centered mostly on weird and funky electrics, he was also interested in the acoustic side of things, albeit from a much more practical standpoint. His 1968 Martin D-35 was his old faithful, his workhorse, his Trigger. But Rory was very much aware of the toll that life on the road can take on an instrument. The '61 Strat was repaired and refretted countless times, but as a solidbody—especially with a bolt-on neck—it could take a beating and then some. An acoustic like the D-35 is another story altogether, especially given Rory's relentless touring. To preserve his most cherished flat-top, he needed a suitable replacement for live work.

That quest was also a sign of the times. In the early 1980s, the acoustic-electric guitar was a well-established concept and brands like Ovation and Takamine were pushing the envelope, trying to get as much tone and volume as possible from acoustic guitars without catching feedback. Even the biggest acoustic-oriented singer/songwriters of the 1960s and 1970s were switching over to more modern designs after years of playing prewar Martins. Acoustic-electrics were also getting easier to play after years of struggling with baseball bat–like necks and high actions. Taylor had introduced a much slimmer neck on their acoustics as early as 1976, and many other brands were starting to catch up.

Washburn Tanglewood

Rory bought his Washburn Tanglewood model around 1981 and put it to good use on the tour in support of the *Jinx* album (1982). As early as January 1982, he can be seen playing it in open G with a capo on the second fret for "Ride On Red, Ride On."

Washburn is one of the oldest guitar brands in the US, established in 1883 in Chicago. They were instrumental in inventing the acoustic guitar as we know it today and were among the first US brands to manufacture their instruments in Japan and Korea in the mid-1970s. The Tanglewood model (not to be confused with the British brand of the same name) was Washburn's attempt to get away from conventional acoustic designs and try something different with the sharp Florentine cutaway and oval soundhole. The preamp system was impressive enough that stars of the era were getting hip to the Tanglewood, including none other than Bob Dylan, who used one in the first half of the 1980s. The slim and highly playable neck probably helped too.

Rory seemed to genuinely enjoy playing his Washburn. He saw it as more than just a good stage tool, using it in the studio in 1987 to record the last track of his *Defender* album, "Seven Days." This beautiful acoustic track with a sparse arrangement closes a loud and busy electric album, and the Washburn in open G is front and center. The guitar shows the love it has received, with a massive scratch below the soundhole, mismatched bridge pins, and missing knob for the preamp. The Washburn wasn't just a temporary replacement for the Martin, it was an instrument with its own voice, one worthy of being captured on record.

Takamine

Takamine Dreadnought

This Takamine is by far the most traditional-looking acoustic bought by Rory to try to replace his good old Martin D-35 for touring. He found it secondhand during his February 1991 Japanese tour and fell in love with both its unplugged and acoustic-electric sounds, even going as far as describing it as "as close to the Martin as I've heard."

Takamine is a Japanese company founded in 1959, but they really hit their stride in the 1970s by exporting well-made acoustic guitars to the US market. Their earlier models were blatant Martin copies, down to the look-alike logo, but over time they created their own visual identity. The true Takamine revolution came in 1978 when they released the Palathetic pickup, a system that included an individual piezo pickup for each string. The result sounded miles ahead of the other acoustic-electric guitars in terms of realism and dynamic range, and many rock stars switched over to Takamine, including the Eagles and Bruce Springsteen.

This dreadnought looks extremely traditional. It doesn't have a cutaway or fancy inlays. It even has the same neck binding as Rory's D-35. A full preamp with EQ sliders makes it as stage-ready as can be. Rory took a liking to it, and he was still using it on tour when he played his last shows in the Netherlands in early 1995. At that point, the setlist included a beautiful acoustic section featuring "Out on the Western Plains," "Walkin' Blues," "Amazing Grace," and "Don't Think Twice, It's Alright," establishing the Takamine as a solid workhorse indeed.

Charvel 625C

Rory went to some strange places in his quest for the perfect guitar to replace his Martin D-35 on stage. Not many guitarists would think of Charvel as an acoustic guitar brand. The California company, founded by Wayne Charvel in the mid-1970s, is closely associated with Floyd Rose–equipped Superstrats used by glam metal shredders such as Warren DeMartini (Ratt) and Jake E. Lee (Ozzy Osbourne). It has made a name by offering instruments with flashy visuals and screaming humbucking pickups—not exactly a first choice for Celtic blues fingerpicking.

But it seems that Rory could find something he liked in any instrument. The 625C was part of a series of cheaper Korean instruments made by Charvel in the 1990s to conquer the booming post–MTV booming acoustic market. Its design is certainly striking, with a rounded mini jumbo body, a cutaway, and the end of the fretboard suspended over the soundhole. The wedge-shaped headstock design is shared with Surfcaster electrics of the same era, and the classic Charvel logo looks out of place on this abalone-ridden acoustic. As could be expected, the neck is extremely slim, and there's a preamp on the side, complete with a three-band EQ.

Rory can be seen playing the Charvel in a few pictures, but judging from the small amount of wear on the guitar, it seems that he went back to the Takamine after a few shows.

Beautiful Weirdos

1983 Tokai Talbo Blazing Fires
1964 Epiphone Coronet
1959 Gibson Les Paul Junior
1959 Gretsch Chet Atkins PX6121
1957 and 1963 Supro Dual Tones
1965 Airline "J.B. Hutto"
1960 Kay K672 Swingmaster
1968 Mosrite Joe Maphis Double Neck
1968 Coral 3S19 Sitar

Talbo
Tokai
BLAZING FIRE

Talbo

When it came to guitars, Rory Gallagher was extremely open-minded—he played and loved them all. He was not a purist or a traditionalist by any stretch of the imagination and seamlessly navigated from priceless vintage pieces like his '61 and '58 Strats to pawnshop dogs like his heavily modded Silvertone. Sometimes, it can seem like there was no real rhyme or reason to his collection; the only common denominator was his passion for the instruments, and in the 1980s he got into the habit of collecting a growing number of guitars. While the ones that he wanted to use on stage were modified, a few of those lovable weirdos stayed original and were only played in the studio or at home.

1983 Tokai Talbo Blazing Fires

Rory seemed to have a special connection with Japan. He did four tours of the country over the course of his career, and he owned many instruments made by Japanese brands. In fact, the only brand that created a signature model for him was Guyatone.

Tokai was among the most important Japanese guitar brands of the late 1970s. They started out building pianos in the late 1940s, but as musical fashions came and went, they ended up building pitch-perfect replicas of Gibson and Fender electrics in 1977. These instruments became known as the "lawsuit" guitars when the big names tried to protect their ownership of the designs. Stevie Ray Vaughan played a Strat-style Tokai, and Billy F Gibbons (ZZ Top) played one of the company's Les Paul–style guitars.

As pressure grew around lawsuit models, Tokai created their own design in 1982: the Talbo Blazing Fire. "Talbo" stands for Tokai aluminum body, and the guitars used an aluminum alloy called AC-4B. Interestingly, the double-cutaway shape with a large pickguard is not unlike the tulip body of the Rickenbacker Combo 400, which might just be accidental.

Wanting to get their new model in artists' hands, Tokai gifted two Talbos to Rory. These could be early-production models judging by the numbers in the back: 80 for the white one, 100 for the black one. The tagline underneath the model name on the headstock boasts "The New Legend of the Guitar Industry," and the result looks very new indeed, especially the pearly white finish. The back of the neck heel has a massive contour to facilitate access to the upper frets, and the whole back of the body has a beautiful German carve à la Rickenbacker.

The model was available in several finishes that would contrast with the black or white pickguard, including gold and blue, and you could get a rosewood or a maple fretboard. The pickups were either three single-coils with a vibrato (Stratocaster anyone?) or two humbuckers (with black plastic covers featuring the embossed Tokai logo) with a fixed bridge. Rory's white Tokai has the maple fretboard and the Strat-like specs, while his black Tokai has the rosewood fretboard with the humbuckers. The latter was used on the *Fresh Evidence* album in 1990, and the former is heard on the solo on "Road to Hell" off *Defender* (1987), with a lower-octave-doubling effect thrown in for good measure.

Talbo

Talbo

Tokai
BLAZING FIRE
THE NEW LEGEND OF THE GUITAR HISTORY

BLAZING FIRE

1964 Epiphone Coronet

A decidedly strange animal in the guitar realm, the Coronet fully deserved a place in the Rory Gallagher collection. Gibson bought the Epiphone brand in 1957 to eliminate competition, especially with archtop guitars. In 1958, Epiphone got into the solidbody electric game, borrowing a big chunk from the double-cutaway Les Paul Junior playbook in creating the Wilshire, Crestwood, and Coronet. The Coronet was the simplest of the bunch with a single bridge pickup, first a New York mini humbucker then a P-90 starting in 1960. In 1963, a third version appeared with a chrome-covered P-90 and a six-in-line "batwing" headstock in place of the previous more traditional 3×3 headstock.

Rory's Coronet has serial number 194324 and it is presented as a 1963, which makes sense from the chrome P-90 and the headstock, but it actually is a 1964 according to Gibson's shipping ledger, which makes more sense given its chunky neck profile and narrow nut.

Unlike many of Rory's guitars, this one hasn't been tinkered with. Either Rory wanted to collect it and not play it too much, or he loved the P-90 (obviously he did) and was satisfied enough with the bridge's intonation that he didn't need to change anything. In any case, it remains one of the most visually striking guitars in his collection, with what appears to be a gorgeous Pacific Blue finish (Epiphone's equivalent of Gibson's Pelham Blue) that has "yellowed" to green over time. Or maybe it was Inverness Green all along. At the 2024 auction, Bonhams presented the Coronet as having been bought "on the 25th November 1978 in Atlanta, USA."

RORY

Epiphone

1959 Gibson Les Paul Junior

Unlike most of his peers, Rory only occasionally played a "proper" Les Paul, that is, a Standard or a Custom. But it's obvious that the Junior's simplicity and the workmanlike philosophy behind it—not to mention lower price—were dear to him. He owned at least two Juniors, a few Junior-style copies, a Junior-like Epiphone Coronet, and a Melody Maker, as well as a Gretsch Corvette with a bridge P-90.

This 1959 Junior represents the second year of the double-cutaway shape. It is the Cherry Red that was standard on this model, as opposed to the standard dark Sunburst of the previous single-cutaway shape (see Rory's 1958 Junior). Also unlike the 1958 Junior, this one doesn't seem to have been used much. It hasn't been modded apart from the replaced tuners, and it still has the original wraparound bridge and the original knobs. This might have been Rory's attempt at recapturing what he loved about the '58 or complementing it with a close cousin.

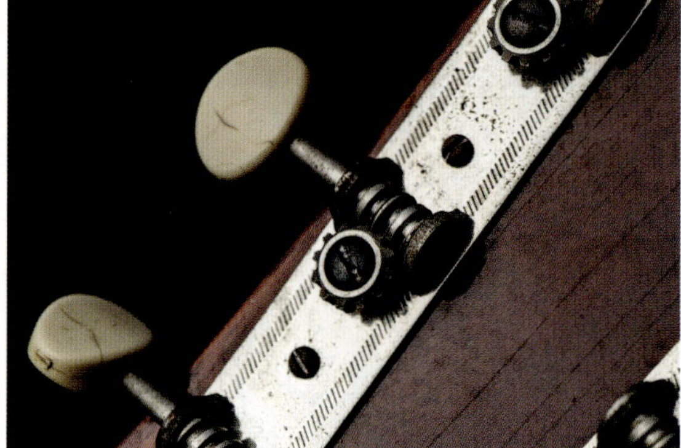

Gibson

1959 Gretsch Chet Atkins PX6121

Fresh Evidence is an extremely special album in Rory Gallagher's discography. This was to be his last album, and even though he would live five more years, he knew his health was failing. Whether he was consciously trying to record his swan song or whether he had just grown tired of the hard rock sound of his last two albums remains a mystery, but one thing is clear: he spent a lot of time recording *Fresh Evidence* and made sure it was the best it could be. Most of his albums before that were attempts to capture the live show and would take as little as two weeks to record. *Fresh Evidence* took no less than six months. It is musically diverse and features many extra musicians, including the return of Lou Martin on piano and Geraint Watkins on accordion.

The change in production is radical, with more organic crunchy guitar sounds that truly showcase the personalities of the instruments Rory used, including a few guitars that were unusual for him, like the '58 Junior and this Gretsch 6121. Rory was not a traditional Gretsch player. After all, he had turned his Corvette into a Les Paul Junior in all but name. But this time, it seems he wanted to use this 6121 for "that great Gretsch sound:" thin, biting, hollow, and twangy. It works particularly well with the tape echo (probably a Watkins Copicat) and spring reverb that are very present in the mix. Rory enjoyed the sound so much that he did not feel the need to modify the guitar.

Gretsch started out in Brooklyn back in 1883, but their prominence in the guitar market emerged in 1954 when they signed an artist deal with country fingerstyle superstar Chet Atkins, who was to be Gretsch's answer to Gibson's Les Paul.

The 6120 was Chet Atkins' first Gretsch, a massive hollowbody with two DynaSonic single-coil pickups and a Bigsby vibrato. Its original transparent orange hue accentuating the wood below became synonymous with the

GRETSCH
GRETSCH
GRETSCH
BY
Bigsby

model. In 1955, the much rarer 6121 was introduced as the semi-solid version of the 6120, with the same shape and structure as the Duo Jet but with the same color and western inlays as its bigger sibling. In 1956, the leather around the body disappeared, then the G-brand on the top. In 1958, Filter'Tron humbucker pickups were introduced in place of the DynaSonics. Finally, in 1961, the 6121 got the same double-cutaway shape as the Duo Jet of the era, but that version is incredibly rare.

This is the main rhythm guitar for the songs "The King of Zydeco" and "Middle Name," and Rory definitely sounds different on those songs, bouncier somehow. We would have loved to hear more of that new direction.

Chet Atkins

1957 and 1963 Supro Dual Tones

As a fan of pawnshops and roots music, it only made sense that Rory would get into Supro guitars. Along with National, Supro was one of the two brands manufactured by Chicago giant Valco in the 1950s. Supros of the era are weird, funky, sometimes outrageous, and often gaudy. And best of all, they have a unique sound that goes well with that unique look.

The Dual Tone was one of Supro's most popular models, and it went through a few iterations. It started out in 1954 as a tiny guitar covered in fake mother of pearl, a material known in guitar circles as mother of toilet seat (basically sparkling plastic), and it got its name from its two pickups. In 1956, the model got its classic white-with-black-pickguard look, its incredibly cool art deco bridge, and a plastic body covering made of a material called No-Mar. This is the version made famous by rock 'n' roll pioneer Link Wray. The Dual Tone got a bigger body in 1958, and finally a new shape with a small second cutaway on the bass side in 1963. That last version has a body made of Res-O-Glas, basically hollow fiberglass that makes it particularly light and resonant.

Rory's dual Dual Tones are great examples of their respective eras. He bought the '57 in 1984, then in 1985 Canadian slide wizard Paul Fenton gifted him the '63 as a thank you for inspiring him to get serious about music at a show twelve years prior. Rory seemed to enjoy the gift, and he used it a few times on stage, mostly for slide of course. The two guitars are quite well-preserved. The '57 has some wear, especially on the copper-plated bridge and pickups. Incidentally, those are single-coil pickups in spite of their appearance.

The '63 has some beautiful greening on the neck pickup, and the material under the Res-O-Glas is starting to appear in the treble-side cutaway thanks to a crack there, maybe caused by a few hits from Rory's bottlenecks.

Dual
Tone

Dual
Tone

Supro

Supro

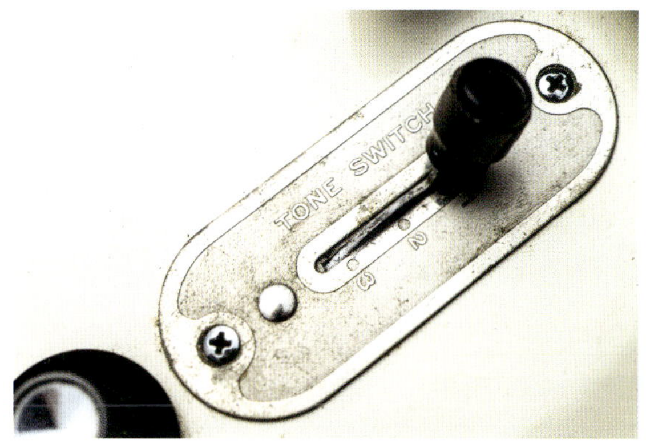
TONE SWITCH

1965 Airline "J.B. Hutto"

The Airline J.B. Hutto has a different brand name, but it came out of the same Valco factory in Chicago as Rory's Supros and is made of the same fiberglass Res-O-Glas material as his 1963 Dual Tone.

The Airline brand was a name created by Montgomery Ward and manufactured by several other brands, just like Silvertone for Sears, Roebuck and Co. Even though that red and white model is most often referred to as the "J.B. Hutto model" as a tribute to the Chicago blues musician of the 1950s and 1960s known for playing it, it was in fact marketed as the Airline Res-O-Glas.

Rory, being the blues connoisseur that he was, must have been aware of the connection when he bought the guitar in 1982. He used it at the 1985 Montreux Jazz Festival (a truly memorable Rory performance in its entirety) to play "I Wonder Who." The model was relatively unknown at the time, but Jack White has since turned it into an icon for a new generation of blues enthusiasts. As is often the case, Rory was there first!

1960 Kay K672 Swingmaster

The Swingmaster is a vastly different beast from the Value Leader previously mentioned. It also falls into the pawnshop guitar category but is a big hollowbody archtop with beautiful art deco appointments such as the triangular headstock logo (with the iconic K) and the wedge tailpiece. The model was the result of a falling out in 1960 between West Coast jazz genius and session man extraordinaire Barney Kessel and Kay executives. When Kay stopped production of their Barney Kessel model, the brand needed a new jazz box, so they recycled ideas from Kessel's model in more discrete packages known as Swingmasters. The two models were made from 1961 to 1965, including the K672 presented here and its upscale sibling, the three-pickup K673.

Rory must have been aware of the Barney Kessel connection, and he probably liked the look and originality of the design, too, but it might have been the pickups that drew him to the Swingmaster. Nicknamed "Kleenex Box" pickups for their appearance, they were actually P-35s and close single-coil cousins

to Gibson's P-90. In fact, P-35s were actually wired for Kay at the Gibson factory!

Rory's last album, 1990's *Fresh Evidence*, has at least four different sleeve artworks depending on the country and the pressing. On some, this K672 appears on the back cover, which could be an indication that he used it on some tracks from the album. A close observation of the f-holes reveals gray foam stuffed inside the body, a classic trick to prevent uncontrollable feedback. This means Rory must have at least plugged it a few times and played it loud enough to realize it needed that fix.

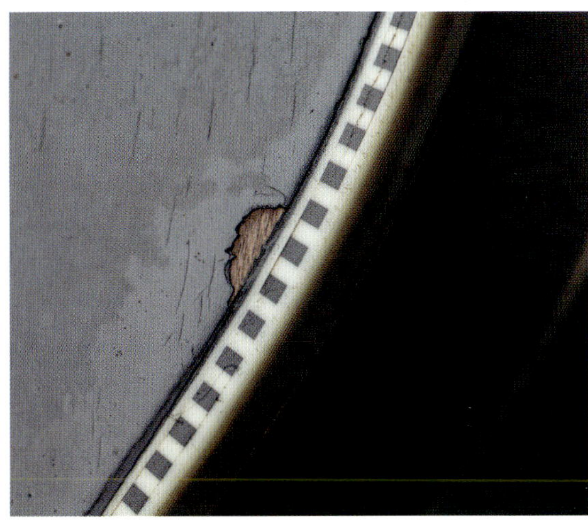

1968 Mosrite Joe Maphis Double Neck

A double-neck guitar seems quite out of place on Rory Gallagher. It feels too grandiose, too cliché for an artist whose stage outfit was the same clothes he wore every day. Rory never wore makeup on stage, never fancied himself a dark wizard or a voodoo priest, and his choice of guitars followed suit with his utilitarian '61 Strat, the Martin D-35, and his Telecasters. Therefore, it is surprising to find a double-neck in his collection, and it obviously couldn't be a classic Gibson EDS-1275 (the SG double-neck). In fact, it probably is the weirdest and most unusual double-neck you could think of: the Mosrite Joe Maphis.

Mosrite is a California brand founded by Semie Moseley, who started out learning his craft under Roger Rossmeisl at Rickenbacker. In 1956, Reverend Ray Boatright helped him create his own brand, hence the Mosrite name for Moseley and Boatright. Country guitar virtuoso Joe Maphis lived nearby in Bakersfield, and his reputation as "King of the Strings" made him the perfect endorsee for the new brand. Moseley began work on a double-neck instrument for Maphis, first with a second neck that was small like a mandolin, and later with a regular twelve-string neck. Moseley designed a shape that became synonymous with his brand, including a longer lower cutaway, an offset waist, slanted pickups, and a traditional German carve contour around the body, a technique he picked up from Rossmeisl.

Rory may not have been aware, but Jimi Hendrix used a Joe Maphis double neck to record "Spanish Castle Magic," even though he never appeared on stage with that strange contraption. Rory never played it live either, but the broken-off vibrato and the extra strap pin in the back mean he must have spent some quality time maneuvering it.

mosrite
mosrite

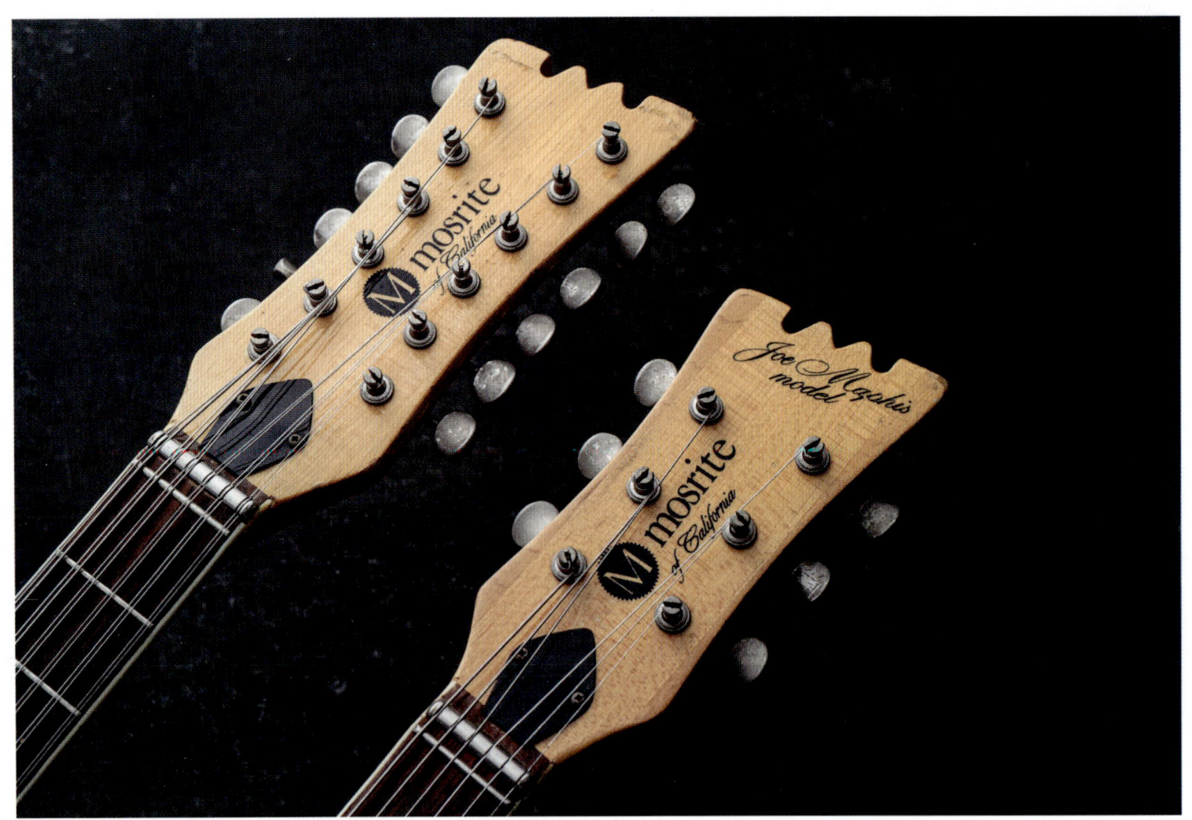

mosrite
of California
Joe Maphis
model
mosrite
of California

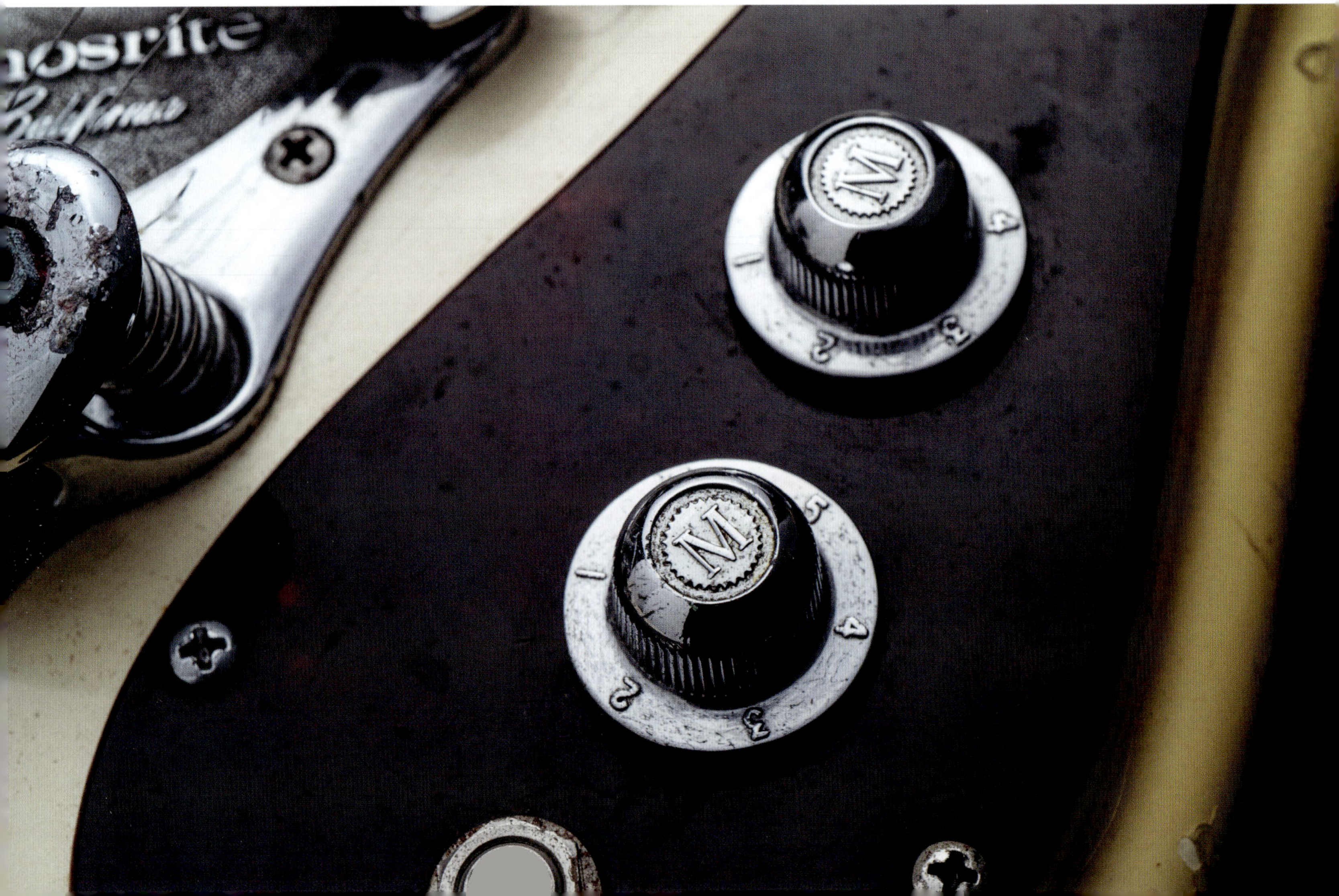
mosrite

mosrite
of California
MOSELEY

1968 Coral 3S19 Sitar

Rory Gallagher wasn't big on changing guitars live. No matter what guitar he had used for recording a song in the studio, he would end up playing it on his good old Strat. The fact that he would jump through hoops to bring a Coral sitar on tour for just one song shows how dedicated he was to replicating "Philby" properly. It wasn't just any song, either: "Philby" (off 1979's *Top Priority*) is about Kim Philby, a British spy who worked for Moscow. Far from giving a history lesson, Rory uses the spy as a metaphor for feeling estranged and remote from one's self.

To give the track a Russian balalaika-like sound, he borrowed a Coral sitar from the Who's Pete Townshend. It was a strange instrument and pretty hard to come by at the time. The Coral brand was created in 1967 when the MCA corporation bought Danelectro and mostly used it to sell more unusual guitars. Vincent Bell was a session guitarist who played on albums by Bob Dylan and Frank Sinatra, among many others. He needed a way to imitate the sound of a sitar, an Indian instrument very much in fashion in mid-1960s western music, without having to learn how to play it. He devised the concept of the electric sitar, basically a regular guitar with a bridge that causes the strings to buzz and thirteen extra sympathetic strings for added resonance (these are not actually played). The Vinnie Bell Coral sitar was a great one-trick pony, and it can be heard on many albums across genres. Bell also designed a twelve-string guitar with a smaller bouzouki-like body that he called the Danelectro Bellzouki, which Rory also had in his collection.

After the *Top Priority* album was released, Rory rented the Coral sitar from Townshend to replicate the song on stage, and it can be heard on a 1979 London broadcast. But the long-term rental started to cost a fortune, so

Coral SITAR
Vincent Bell

Dónal Gallagher searched for a Coral to buy. Rory passed on one in Australia (he played an extensive tour there in June 1980) because it was too expensive. As Dónal recalls, "He was hiring the Coral sitar from the Who enterprise, it was a Pete Townshend instrument. Rory's paying a lot of money per day, he's used it on the record, and he went off for a world tour. He knew this was gonna cost so much, especially with insurance and travel. I saw one down in Australia and the guy turned up in Melbourne. It would have been even rarer there than in Europe. But he was asking too much so Rory didn't buy it even though that meant he would have to keep hiring the one from the Who."

This is probably why he's seen playing "Philby" on his '61 Strat during a concert in Zurich later in 1980: to stop overspending for just one song. As luck would have it, Dónal finally found one in New Jersey for the princely sum of $1,500 (close to $6,000 in today's money!) and bought it, thereby ending the rental. He returned to London aboard the Concorde and had to pay extra taxes on his new acquisition at British customs, turning "Philby" into a decidedly expensive song! Incidentally, Dónal recalls bumping into Cliff Richard who had done a show in New York the night before, which makes it fairly easy to date the purchase since the British singer, who did not perform in New York often, had a show at the New York Savoy in April 1981. This lines up with Rory being back on a Coral sitar for "Philby" on his 1982 Rockpalast performance, as well as the 1985 Montreux Jazz Festival show. The Coral sitar might be the only guitar that Rory regularly played on stage without ever modifying it. It was already perfect for what it needed to be.

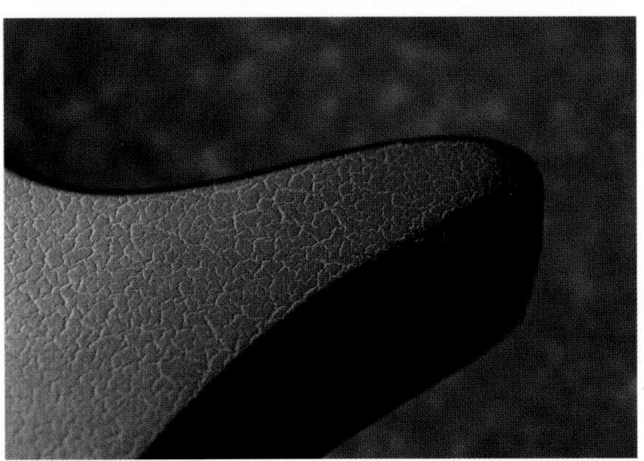

1991-1995

Rory's Last Stand

The Final Session

1965 Teisco TRE-100
1960s Stella Harmony H912

OFF ↔ ON
MODEL

MODEL
TBL-00

Rory was never one to phone it in. He played every show with an intensity that made it feel special. It was the same at the studio, especially toward the end of Rory's life, when his recordings became more laid-back, with deeper production.

Even for a project as dubious as the tribute album that would turn out to be his last session, he went all in. *Rattlesnake Guitar: The Music of Peter Green* (1995) was a tribute to the great Fleetwood Mac founder who had artistically been flying under the radar since the early 1970s. Green, who was coping with mental health issues and was detached from his musical past, did not take part in the album. But Rory delivered, and how, choosing two obscure songs in the Green catalog. "Leaving Town Blues" is an outtake from the band's early stages released on the 1971 compilation album *The Original Fleetwood Mac*, and "Show Biz Blues" is a deep cut from the third Fleetwood Mac album (and last with Peter Green), 1969's *Then Play On*. Those superb performances could have been part of the *Fresh Evidence* sessions, with Rory displaying an unprecedented level of musical wisdom, playing fewer notes and leaving a lot of room for the music to breathe.

1965 Teisco TRE-100

For the recording of "Show Biz Blues," it seems like Rory wanted to continue exploring the musical road he had started to travel down on tracks like "The King of Zydeco" from *Fresh Evidence*, relying on interesting guitar sounds that would make the part. The arrangement is sparse and the repeated rhythm makes the song deeply hypnotic. The guitar is not really a rhythmic element: it holds long notes, plays stabs, and sometimes makes its presence felt by not playing at all. The unusual guitar sound has a movement to it, which could be the built-in harmonic tremolo from an old Magnatone amp (Rory had a Magnatone 190 that can be seen in publicity shots for *Fresh Evidence*) or the vibrato from the BOSS VB-2 pedal (which Rory owned too). There's more dirt on the sound, a fuzzier edge than on most of Rory's recordings, and it's all courtesy of an extremely weird guitar: a 1965 Teisco TRE-100 (also sold as Silvertone's 1487 model). The pictures of the recording show him playing with a capo on the fifth fret and the song is in C, which most likely meant the guitar was tuned to open G.

Teisco was yet another Japanese brand, and the TRE-100 had been made famous by Chicago bluesman Hound Dog Taylor. The guitar was an unusual instrument even by Teisco's quirky standards: it had a built-in amp! The extra growth on the treble side of the body hides a speaker underneath the pick-guard, and the whole thing is activated with the on/off switch on the bass side. There was also a TRE-110 model with a built-in tremolo. Those battery-powered transistor amps would overheat pretty easily though, and most have been nonfunctioning for decades by now.

There's also a "regular" jack output that by-passes the built-in amp and allows the player to enjoy the clear bright sound of the Teisco single-coil pickup. These "gold foil" pickups, so-called for their covers, have seen a strong resurgence as of late. Yet again, Rory was way ahead of the curve on this one.

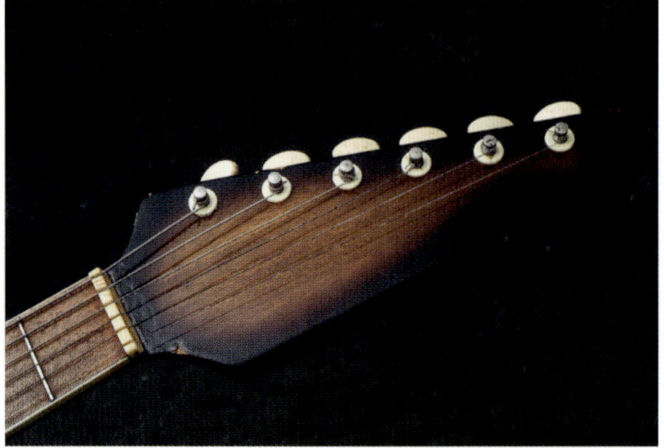

MODEL

OFF ↔ ON

Stella
HARMONY

1960s Stella Harmony H912

In a fitting full-circle moment, one of the last guitars Rory Gallagher played in the studio and on TV was an obvious tribute to one of the greatest blues and folk singers that ever was, Lead Belly. Huddie Ledbetter's recordings have allowed many traditional folk songs to survive to the present day, and over the course of his career Rory covered some of those songs. The most obvious is "Out on the Western Plains" off 1975's *Against the Grain*, but on Taste's debut album he also covered "Leavin' Blues." Lead Belly was part of Rory's universe from the beginning.

Lead Belly played a twelve-string Stella, a cheaper brand belonging to the Oscar Schmidt Company of New Jersey. In the 1920s, their twelve-string models had a longer scale than usual (26.5 inches) to accommodate lower tunings. The lush and deep sound of Lead Belly's down-tuned twelve-string was the perfect orchestra to accompany his stentorian voice.

Rory's Stella was built in the 1960s, by which time the brand belonged to the Chicago company Harmony. Rory used the Stella to record "Leaving Town Blues" for the 1995 Peter Green tribute album that would represent his last session. This is also the guitar he used for his last TV appearance, in 1994 for the Irish channel UTV. The opening shot of the segment shows him playing the Stella with a few other guitars in the background: the Teisco TRE-100 that he also used for the Peter Green tribute sessions, the Charvel 625C acoustic, and the black Esquire without its middle pickup—all of them like different sides of a lifetime's devotion to the blues.

Stella
HARMONY

Epilogue

Rory's Legacy

Rory Gallagher was the ultimate underdog. He never was a bestselling artist, none of his albums ever hit the top of the charts, and he rarely released singles, yet his back catalog has remained in demand. And he at least partly influenced fellow all-time greats of the guitar world, including Hendrix, Page, Gilmour, Clapton, and the like. He was not a larger-than-life or mysterious guitarist, but an incredibly talented lover of the blues who wanted to share his enthusiasm with the world.

Many of his admirers went on to have extremely successful careers. Brian May from Queen got his sonic recipe from Rory's rig. Judas Priest, Def Leppard, and Iron Maiden got a lot of mileage from Rory's lyrical lead playing. And Johnny Marr of the Smiths took Rory's approach and did something completely different with it. Rory also did a lot to put Ireland on the musical map, and he was instrumental in opening the rock business's gates for artists like Thin Lizzy, Gary Moore, and U2.

In fact, American guitar hero Joe Bonamassa played two shows in Cork in mid-2025 to commemorate the thirtieth anniversary of Rory's passing.

While Rory's influence on many top-tier guitarists is undeniable, he has also had a major role in the guitar industry by virtue of his inseparable '61 Strat. Nowadays, it seems that wear and tear on an older instrument makes it more desirable, a romantic notion that has spawned a whole segment of the guitar market that started in the 1990s. "Relic" guitars have been made to look worn out of the factory, from Fender's affordable Mexican-made Road Worn series to Gibson's meticulous top-dollar replicas of each and every ding on famous instruments.

The Fender Custom Shop has been building the Rory Gallagher Stratocaster since 1997, making it the longest-running artist signature in the Custom Shop line and the first really popular model in the Relic Series. In fact, it is one of the rare signature models that never existed in a non-relic version, since the original guitar is defined by its battle scars more than anything else.

Rory knew a battered guitar could be a superior instrument long before anybody else had the notion. In the 1970s and 1980s, many players were paying to have their '50s Strats refinished. The executives at Fender had no idea why Rory would want to play on that old piece of rotting wood. According to legend, they were embarrassed that Rory's Strat was representing their bestselling model—so much so that in November 1979, they gave him a brand-new guitar. It was the Strat designed by Fender for the model's twenty-fifth anniversary, one of the very first off the production line with the faulty white finish. As Dónal Gallagher recalls:

> *We were doing a TV thing leading up to the twenty-fifth anniversary, I think it was* BBC Sights and Sounds, *and the American Fender guys from CBS were there. At the time, they had an ad with Buddy Holly, Jimi Hendrix, and Rory, and they gave him the Silver Strat. The serial number was 004, since Fender would keep two for their archive. Rory was the first musician to get one. Then, six months later, I got a call from Fender saying, "We want the guitar back to have it resprayed." The finish was starting to look like crocodile skin. Rory said "No, that guitar is not going anywhere." I didn't understand, but he knew that respraying it would make it less collectible.*

Rory was a precursor of the relic decades before Stevie Ray Vaughan, a pawnshop guitar aficionado decades before Jack White, and a genuine lover of any instrument that could bring him any kind of inspiration.

1978 Ibanez MC500DS

1964 Burns Bison

1980 Veillette Citron Shark

1990 National Resophonic

1964 Silvertone S1478L

1960 Supro Coronado

1960 Danelectro Bellzouki 12-String

1959 Burns Weill "RP1" Roy Plummer Super Streamline

1981 Musima Elektrina

Non-Auction Instruments

The instruments of the 2024 Bonhams auction are not a full representation of the guitars that Rory acquired across the years. The guitars on the pages that follow are a partial representation of Rory's non-auction instruments. *Photos by Shu Tomioka*

Late-1950s Barth Model 200

1960 Silvertone 1323

1963 Gretsch Corvette PX6135

1964 Epiphone Casino

1964 Gibson Melody Maker

1965 Guild S-200 Thunderbird

1967 Danelectro 5025 Convertible

1971 Eccleshall
Electric Mandola

1974 Gibson L6-S Deluxe

1976 Fender Stratocaster

1976 Yamaha SX800B

1977 Guyatone Glory LG1000
Deluxe Prototype

1979 25th Anniversary Fender
Stratocaster S/N 000004

1979 Ibanez MC500DS
Musician

1979 Ibanez ST300

1980 Ibanez V302BS

1980 Sigma DM5

1980s Dave Edwards Custom Fender Stratocaster

1980s Giffin Q7

1980s–1990s Fender Component Telecaster

1980s–1990s Fender Component Telecaster

1980s–1990s Fender Component Telecaster

1980s–1990s Fender Component Telecaster

1980s–1990s Fender Component Telecaster

1981 Fender Lead

1980s The Gibson Les Paul Junior

1990 Charvel Surfcaster

1990s Höfner 500/1 V63

1990s Hohner L90 Professional

1991 Patrick Eggle JS Berlin Legend

1991 Guyatone "Marroly" LGX-II Prototype

1992 Fender La Brea

1993 Gibson Nighthawk Custom

1993 Cheri T-Style

Image Captions

4 On March 26, 1976, Rory was photographed in the Netherlands with some of his favorite things for the cover of *The Best of Rory Gallagher. Photo by Govert De roos*

9 Rory performs with Taste . . . prior to dropping the definitive article. Pictured are bassist Richard McCracken and drummer John Wilson. *Photofest*

16 Rory and his '61 in the studio. It was the last year for the slab fretboard, which would be replaced by inferior veneer. Rory had long since dispensed with the tremolo arm. *Photofest*

31 The Rangemaster in action, perched atop Rory's Vox AC30. The distinct striped awning identifies the venue as London's famed Marquee Club. *Dónal Gallagher/Strange Music Ltd.*

39 The sound of Bjärnum. The Swedish entry in Rory's collection had a small parlor-size body and a twelve-fret neck with a large V profile. *Photographer unknown/Strange Music Ltd.*

43 Rory plays the Italian mandolin at Belgium's Jazz Bilzen festival, August 21, 1971. *Photo by Laurens Van Houten, courtesy Frank White Photo Agency*

55 Rory experimented with middle- and neck-position blade pickups in the '66 Tele from 1979 to the early 1980s but reverted to a somewhat original configuration. *John Minihan/Strange Music Ltd.*

56 The white Tele's main claim to fame is Taste's appearance at the August 28, 1970, Isle of Wight concert. *Photographer unknown/Strange Music Ltd.*

59 The white Tele was one of Rory's main instruments and the third most expensive electric sold at the 2024 auction. *Michael Ochs Archives/Getty Images*

61 Rory's Esquire features a top-loading bridge, a design that appears only on late-1958 and early-1959 Teles and Esquires. P*hotographer unknown/Strange Music Ltd.*

68 The Esquire makes an appearance at the Royal Albert Hall, London, on December 23, 1975. *Photo by Gus Stewart/Redferns/Getty Images*

71 Channeling Chuck Berry in Amsterdam, October 19, 1974. *Photo by Laurens Van Houten, courtesy Frank White Photo Agency*

76 Rory used the Martin at a Sydney press conference to help promote February 1975 Australian tour dates. *Photo by Gregory Lee/Fairfax Media via Getty Images*

79 In 1975, Rory told *Melody Maker*, "When I first got the Martin, I've gotta say that I was a bit disappointed, but as I played it, the guitar seemed to get better." *Photographer unknown/Strange Music Ltd.*

84 Rory wasted little time putting the 1930 National to use upon acquiring it in 1930. *Photographer unknown/Strange Music Ltd.*

87 The National accompanied Rory for several important television appearances, as well as live concert dates like this engagement at the Royal Albert Hall on December 23, 1975. P*hoto by Laurens Van Houten, courtesy Frank White Photo Agency*

93 Rory and the A Style mandolin at the Free Trade Hall in Manchester, England, January 17, 1977. *Photo by Steve Smith, via the Rory Gallagher Music Library, Cork*

134 Receiving his signature Guyatone upon arriving at Tokyo in January 1975 was a thrill for Rory. *Photo by Keiko Motohashi/ Strange Music Ltd.*

143 Photographed in studio for the *Top Priority* album cover, June 11, 1979. He plays a Fender Stratocaster guitar. *Photo by Brian Cooke/Redferns/Getty Images*

151 The massive amount of overdrive provided by the Marshall combos meant Rory no longer needed his Rangemaster or Hawk II booster. *Photographer unknown/ Strange Music Ltd.*

159 The 1958 Strat was not one of Rory's most-played guitars, but its status as backup to the '61 spoke volumes for its place in Rory's lineup. *Photographer unknown/Strange Music Ltd.*

165 The Corvette ended up superseding the black Esquire as Rory's main slide guitar in the late 1970s. ***Photographer unknown/ Strange Music Ltd.***

173 Another beautiful weirdo. Rory's 1978 Musicmaster saw some concert action, including this show in Bologna, Italy, on July 1, 1982. *Photo by Luciano Viti/Getty Images*

181 This 1960 Melody Maker entered Rory's world in 1985, and he used it both for slide and also in standard tuning for bluesier numbers. *Photographer unknown/ Strange Music Ltd.*

187 The Takamine Dreadnought in Rory's collection was as unadorned and traditional looking as could be, but it proved a worthy instrument for reproducing acoustic guitar sounds in live settings. *Photo by Stuart Mostyn/Redferns/Getty Images*

189 The condition of the Charvel suggests Rory gigged it only a few times before returning to the Takamine. *Photographer unknown/Strange Music Ltd.*

211 Canadian guitarist Paul Fenton gifted Rory the 1963 Dual Tone in 1985. Rory would go on to use it onstage for slide work. *Photographer unknown/Strange Music Ltd*

215 Rory puts his Airline Res-O-Glas through its paces at Festivalcatraz, Zonhoven, Belgium, on August 4, 1984. *Photo by Gie Knaeps/Getty Images*

227 Dónal's purchase of the Coral sitar obviated the need for Rory to continue the expensive rental of Pete Townshend's for touring. *Photo by Paul Natkin/Getty Images*

229 The Teisco TRE-100—another Japanese brand and another quirky guitar previously made famous by a bluesman, in this case Hound Dog Taylor. *Photographer unknown/Strange Music Ltd.*

238 Rory used the Stella to record "Leaving Town Blues" for the 1995 Peter Green tribute album that would represent his last session. *Photographer unknown/ Strange Music Ltd.*

253 Electric Ballroom, London, 1980. *Photo by David Corio/Redferns/Getty Images*

Index

Acknowledgments

Many thanks to Anna, Ella, Joshua, Eleanor & Chris, Alexandre, Jack, Dónal, and Daniel. And of course David, who turned me on to *Irish Tour '74* two decades ago. —*JB*

Thank you to Dónal and Daniel Gallagher, Julien Bitoun, Chris Vinnicombe, Simon Ayre, Jo Johnson, Claire Tole-Moir, Fred Lawton, Dennis Pernu, and Bob Hewitt for your parts, big and small, in bringing this project to life. —*EJ*

About the Authors

Julien Bitoun is a guitarist, author, content creator, and lecturer. In addition to writing for several guitar magazines, he is the author of a number of books, including *Les Paul: 70 Years, Guitars and Heroes* and *The Story of Woodstock Live: 50 Years*.

Eleanor Jane is a photographer and writer in the music industry who specializes in photographing creative artist portraits and vintage and culturally significant guitars. Eleanor's work has been featured extensively in books and magazines around the world, and she is renowned for her detailed and atmospheric guitar photography, which evokes the spirit of the instrument and the stories it has to tell.

Quarto.com

First Published in 2026 by Motorbooks, an imprint of The Quarto Group,
100 Cummings Center, Suite 265-D, Beverly, MA 01915, USA.
T (978) 282-9590 F (978) 283-2742

EEA Representation, WTS Tax d.o.o.,
Žanova ulica 3, 4000 Kranj, Slovenia.
www.wts-tax.si

30 29 28 27 26   1 2 3 4 5

ISBN: 978-0-7603-9848-7

Digital edition published in 2026
eISBN: 978-0-7603-9849-4

Library of Congress Cataloging-in-Publication Data

Names: Bitoun, Julien author | Parsons, Eleanor Jane photographer
Title: Gallagher's guitars : the Rory Gallagher collection / text by Julien Bitoun ; photography by Eleanor Jane Parsons.
Description: Beverly, MA : Motorbooks, 2026. | Includes index. | Summary: "Gallagher's Guitars provides an intimate look at the instruments of one of the most electrifying guitarists and performers of the rock era" —Provided by publisher.
Identifiers: LCCN 2025032153 | ISBN 9780760398487 | ISBN 9780760398494 ebook
Subjects: LCSH: Gallagher, Rory--Musical instrument collections | Electric guitar--Pictorial works | Guitar--Pictorial works | LCGFT: Illustrated works
Classification: LCC ML419.G25 B58 2026 | DDC 787.87166092--dc23/eng/20250903
LC record available at https://lccn.loc.gov/2025032153

Design and Page Layout: Justin Page
Slipcase Images: Eleanor Jane
Book Cover Image: Pictorial Press Ltd./Alamy Stock Photos

Printed in Guangdong, China TT122025

GHER BAND

RORY GALLA